To Life:
My Miraculous Journey

Sharon Joy Rawitz

© **Copyright 2018**, by Sharon Joy Rawitz

Library of Congress Control Number: 2019908868

Sharon Joy Rawitz resides in New York City. She is available to give motivation talks and meet the author discussions. She can be contacted by email at **circ3mmm@gmail.com.**

Cover Designs: Sharon Joy Rawitz

Artistic Consultant: Dianna Rawitz

Photo Credit: Hershel Baron

Exercises Disclaimer:
The exercises provided in this book are for educational and entertainment purposes only, and are not to be interpreted as a recommendation for a specific treatment plan.

ALWAYS CONSULT YOUR FAMILY PHYSICIAN PRIOR TO INITIATING ANY EXERCISE PROGRAM.

To Life: My Miraculous Journey

Is dedicated to the memory of my sister,
Phillis Ann Maiorella, ob 'm
*who encouraged me to write this book
and physically put my words on paper.*

FORWORD VII
MY SISTER VIII
ACKNOWLEDGMENTS IX
   PREFACE XI
STORY PART ONE 1
   CHAPTER 1 - THE FIRST EPISODE 1
   CHAPTER 2 - STILL ANOTHER EPISODE AND ADMITTED TO THE HOSPITAL 3
      REACTION AT JOB 5
   CHAPTER 3 - NEW YORK UNIVERSITY MEDICAL CENTER 8
   CHAPTER 4 - STROKE UNIT 11
   CHAPTER 5 - REACTIONS TO MEDICATIONS 14
   CHAPTER 6 - SUPPORT OUTSIDE OF HOSPITAL 15
   CHAPTER 7 - RUSK REHABILITATION CENTER: RELEARNING THE ACTIVITIES OF DAILY LIVING 16
   CHAPTER 8 - PHYSICAL THERAPY 21
   CHAPTER 9 - SPEECH THERAPY 24
   CHAPTER 10 - OCCUPATIONAL THERAPY 27
   CHAPTER 11 - EXTRACURRICULAR ACTIVATES 31
   CHAPTER 12 - TISCH 32
   CHAPTER 13 - ANOTHER REHAB FACILITY 34
   CHAPTER 14 - HOME 36
   CHAPTER 15 - USING A TELEPHONE 39
   CHAPTER 16 - VISITING NURSE SERVICES: PHYSICAL, OCCUPATIONAL, AND SPEECH THERAPY AND AN AIDE 42
   CHAPTER 17 - MEDICAL TESTS 47
   CHAPTER 18 - SWIMMING 49
   CHAPTER 19 - MEALS AND MEDS 51
   CHAPTER 20 - DRESSING MYSELF 52
   CHAPTER 21 - STRESS 54
   CHAPTER 22 - REDUCING MEDICATIONS 56
   CHAPTER 23 - NADIVA 58
   CHAPTER 24 - TERRACE FLOWER POT GARDEN 59
   CHAPTER 25 - VIOLIN 61
   CHAPTER 26 - COMPUTER 64
      The American Stroke Association tells us about that: 66
      Wernicke's Aphasia (receptive) 66
      Broca's Aphasia (expressive) 67
   CHAPTER 27 - MORE SPEECH THERAPY 69
   CHAPTER 28 - TRANSPORTATION 72
   CHAPTER 29 - FEELING THE STRESS 74
   CHAPTER 30 - MY FEELINGS THIS MORNING 76
   CHAPTER 31 - SPIRITUALITY 80
PART TWO 83
   CHAPTER 1 - OPPORTUNITIES FOR JEWISH LEARNING; LEARNING WITH ESTHER 83
   CHAPTER 2 - THE LIBRARY 86
   CHAPTER 3 - WALKING WITH PAIN 87
   CHAPTER 4 - ALTERNATIVE TECHNIQUES 92
   CHAPTER 5 - TEACHING DANCE 96
   CHAPTER 6 - WATCHING MY GRANDDAUGHTER 98
   CHAPTER 7 - ACCESS-A-RIDE 102
   CHAPTER 8 - CERTIFICATE OF OCCUPANCY 104

CHAPTER 9 - SPRING 2008 GARDEN	108
CHAPTER 10 - TEVYE THE MILKMAN (A/K/A FIDDLER ON THE ROOF)	109
CHAPTER 11 - THE AMEN GROUP	110
CHAPTER 12 - PHYSICAL PROGRESS	112
CHAPTER 13 - HEALTH INSURANCE AND TREATMENT	116

PART THREE 120

SUMMING UP 2-13-13	120

PERSPECTIVES OF FAMILY MEMBERS AND FRIENDS 128

MICHAEL RAWITZ	128
LILA BAIDA	133
MIKE BARNETT	133
FAYA COHEN	134
LORI MARTON	136
PAMELA ECKHAUS	137
SYBIL SIDELMAN RYAN	139
DEB HIRSCHHORN	140
NINA FLEISCHMAN	141

INTERVIEW: 143

MEDICAL RECORDS 152

GLOSSARY 154

PART 1	154
PART 2	155

FORWORD

"The art of living is courageous" is a most appropriate anthem for Sharon's look back and reflection upon a major crisis and the ongoing challenges that have impacted her life and life choices. She has portrayed her challenges so that the reader can imagine stepping into her shoes. It is most courageous to be that exposed.

Sharon takes one on a frightening ride from the abrupt vascular event in her head which left her with the fear of the unknown and loss of control, when just before she had felt in control of her life. She demonstrates her faith in her spiritual bedrock and most importantly, in herself. The detailed explanation of her aphasia illuminates the loneliness and isolation of one who has sustained a major cerebral vascular event. She rejoices in how some people in her world embrace the opportunity to assist and is disappointed by the ignorance of others to her disability.

Sharon is most capable of allowing us to see the investment she has made in her relationships with family and friends. It **was her insight to them, the intellectual awareness of them, and her encompassing personality** that brought them to her side at her time of need. The lesson to be learned is that this level of commitment to family and friends can pay off many times over. Sharon escorts the reader into her emotional, intellectual, and religious communities so we can appreciate the dependency we have on one another. On the one hand, she lets us feel her joy in receiving much needed assistance in a time of need, and her disappointment in the behavior of others who were not as aware of her need for help. Remarkable.

I learned a great deal more about the members of her inner circle. I learned of their level of love and respect for Sharon.

Activities of daily living can at times be enormously challenging. There are real barriers. Sharon has expertly explained this struggle with her own unique perspective. Who knew that these seemingly simple actions could be that tough?

The details that she gives about her difficulties with finances and disability present a cold reality that many of us will never experience. She exposed herself so that the reader could truly know what it was like. Chilling.

The message that I will always carry with me is her expectation to recover and survive. This is an accurate reflection of her enormous personality. What a blessing.

Having the opportunity to participate in her world and life, and now reading her words, has taught me about a remarkably courageous woman.

Submitted July 4, 2017, Stephen A. Smiles, M.D. -- one of Sharon's physicians

Esther Levitt

MY SISTER

She moved her left foot forward

She told her right foot to follow

She taught her left hand to write

She taught her right hand to write

She had the words in her head

She forced them out of her mouth

She looked at all of this as a challenge

She won the battle

My amazing sister

ACKNOWLEDGMENTS

In the process of my recovery and writing this book I owe great thanks to so many:
First and foremost, I thank God who is my loving guide and healer.

I greatly thank my family, sisters, children, and grandchildren, who have lovingly supported and continue to support me in countless ways.

A special thanks to Dr. Stephen Smiles of NYU Medical Center and Rusk Rehabilitation Center who with his knowledge, warmth, understanding, and patience, has and continues to oversee my medical care.

My appreciation goes to the nurses and therapists who worked with me at the Rusk Rehabilitation Center.

A special thanks to my speech therapist who helped me regain my speech post hospital.

Many thanks to Moshe Kranz and Ann Schweiger for their technical support.

Special thanks to Joseph Geller for performing the exercises from the written page to test the clarity of the written instructions.

My appreciation to all those that helped in the editing and proof reading: Esther Levitt, Mimi Samuels, Sarah Silverman, Valerie Roshan, Faya Cohen, Elise Teitelbaum, Rochel Lieberman, Charles Milenka, Rebeka Gutkind and Devorah Cohen.

Last but not least, thanks to my friends and my community, who have been there to offer a helping hand and their prayers for my recovery that warmed my heart.

PREFACE

I am writing about my experience in the hope that it can be helpful to other patients who are still suffering from the effects of a stroke. Many are unable to communicate their feelings and needs to their families, therapists, and doctors. Although these helpers have much knowledge, they seldom have the intimate understanding that comes with first-hand experience. I have been very blessed to have regained my strength and speech and clear thinking. I am anxious to share my own experience and insights with as many people as possible, thereby hopefully easing their pain and aiding in their recovery.

STORY PART ONE

CHAPTER 1 - *The first episode*

Background: dance teacher, writer, social worker, guidance counselor.

It was Friday afternoon, April 15th, 2005. The Busy Buddy Newspaper Club met in my office where they were working on the next edition. At the beginning of the school year I initiated the school newspaper as a school-wide volunteer project. As their school guidance counselor, I saw this as a wonderful opportunity for the students' self-expression while using their academic skills to work together and increase their communication skills while augmenting their self-esteem. I was sitting at my computer when a sharp pain took hold of my head and upper body, I stiffened up. After a pause I walked with great difficulty to a seat beside a table on the other side of the room. Suddenly I realized I was sick; so did the students who were working at another table. They saw my pain. Without hesitation a student brought an assistant principal to help. At first I couldn't move. I couldn't speak. She asked me how I felt. I wanted to say that I was fine, but I was not. She waited till I could speak, maybe ten minutes or more. She told me that I was as white as the toilet tissue beside me on the table and suggested that I go to the hospital in an ambulance. Without too much resistance, I agreed. My sister Esther was called. The emergency medical service was called. My office was on the third floor. The building had no elevator. There was some discussion between the Emergency Medical Technician (EMT) personnel as to how they were going to lower me to the ground level. They spoke of bumping me down the stairs on the wheel chair or sled. I thought to myself this was not going to do. My head was in extreme pain. I could not take any concussive movements. I told them I would rather walk. I was supported on each side by two EMT's as we climbed down the three flights of stairs to the first floor landing. As I passed some of the students I could hear their concern. They said to one another, "I hope Mrs. Rawitz didn't have a stroke."

At the local hospital I was examined and released with no diagnosis -- they said I had a headache. My sister met me at the hospital and drove me home.

During that week this feeling happened repeatedly. I was attending a guidance counselors' meeting at the district office and repeatedly had to excuse myself and suppress my coughing and nausea. Two days later, after work, I went to my computer graphics class in Ozone Park. I was almost there. The pain was like a migraine headache. It was overwhelming. I had to stop the car and could not move. I was nauseated until the episode subsided. I had no idea what was happening. I was moments away from my class. Should I go or should I turn back? Maybe the episode was over and I could continue my studies. I found the class challenging and rewarding. I took off my hat and coat and sat down on my seat and turned on the computer to the scene I had been working on. I tried to hold back the vomit but it was no use. I stumbled off to the ladies' room. My head was reeling. My stomach gave out. I went back to the classroom and excused myself. I shut down my computer, put on my coat, and got to my car. I managed to stay focused for the next thirty minutes till I arrived home.

The headaches continued.

CHAPTER 2 - Still another episode and admitted to the hospital

Spring break

While visiting with friends for dinner the first night of Passover (Saturday, April 23, 05) the sound of their voices became overwhelming in my head. It was as if I was moving into an unfamiliar place. My eyes felt very strange. As they were speaking my right eye felt especially strange. It felt as if a curtain of bright light was very slowly enveloping me. I was fascinated by it. The brilliance was beautiful.

I kept looking in wonder and awe at the brilliance of the light. My friends noticed the strange expression on my face. I was silent. They realized something was very wrong and called the Hatzala Ambulance. They were there in two minutes. I had no speech while this was happening. Until this time I was very healthy. I had a full time job. I had many interests. I was physically fit. My life just changed.

The ambulance people asked my age. I told them I was twenty-six. I was reversing numbers. Could they have believed me because of my physical fitness (ha ha) or was it just the routine to check the state of my brain function? My friend's daughter accompanied me to the hospital. When I saw the emergency room sign from the ambulance I blacked out. It was the last thing I saw. I was told that my friend's daughter stayed with me all night. She undressed me and saw to it that I was tended.

My family was called and came. I was unconscious. I have no memory of the next three days. My family told me that I tried to get out of the hospital; I would run down the hall trying to leave. The staff didn't seem to notice. At my family's request, I was put in restraints. I was talking a blue streak to them. It was obvious to me that I knew what I was saying, but all that was heard by others was "ya da ya da ya da ya da".

It was twenty-four hours before I was even given a bed.

When I awoke from this unconscious state, my arms were flailing, fighting the restraints. My family was there and removed the ties. My son Michael told me that I appeared to be in a lot of pain and that I was trying to express myself but didn't make any sense.

I can't remember the first room they put me in. At this time I was hyper-sensitive to light and sound and had to have the blinds closed. Michael told me that the first room had two beds but I was the only patient in the room.

The doctors first diagnosed me with Meningitis and kept me isolated. Then they realized it was not Meningitis. They had no idea what I had or how to treat me. I had a very high fever. The doctor prescribed Tylenol every 4 to 6 hours rectally, because I did not have the ability to swallow. The nurse came in and tried to give me a Tylenol orally. If my family were not there to stop her I probably would have choked on the Tylenol. I have been told that there were many incidents of this nature which occurred at the Peninsula Hospital. I was then moved from room to room. An aide came to the room; she opened the blinds, and my eyes and my head started to throb. I told her that it was bothering me and to please close the blind. She insisted that the light was wonderful. She was totally insensitive to my needs. I wound up screaming, crying with pain, till the nurse came in and interceded. The nurse said that if there was a problem I should tell her. Too bad; the problem should not have been in the first place. With assistance I was able to walk to the bathroom. I am a very independent person. They tried to give me a bedpan. I was very uncomfortable. It seemed to me it would be easier for them to simply walk with me to the bathroom. I guess that I was wrong about that. My balance was off but with assistance I was able to do this. However a particular aide decided I no longer needed assistance and would no longer hold my arm. I found that to be frightening.

My daughter Dianna and my four year old grandson, Luca, from Canada, had visited me a few weeks before this occurrence. It was always a treat to visit with them. Luca at four years old loved to take pictures. He knew how to use both a regular and digital camera. We walked to the beach and played ball and enjoyed the sights and sounds. Then, just a short time later, Dianna was back without Luca, this time to take care of me in the hospital. She kept me company and helped me with my balance when I walked. She took care of my mail at home. She sorted and took care of my bills. It was great to have her close to me in body and soul, but her husband Franc and son Luca missed her.

After a week Dianna had to return home, but I still had a lot of help. I can't imagine how people who are incapacitated are able to manage without a support network of family and friends. My neighbors came to visit and helped take my mind off my physical problems. They made me smile and laugh and brought me home-made goodies.

REACTION AT JOB

All this happened at the beginning of the spring Passover/Easter break. Because we had the break the students and faculty were unaware of my condition until a week and a half later when they came back from vacation; even then sometimes people extended their vacation time and came back late to work. My sister Esther had been in touch with my school to let them know that I was in the hospital; it was serious and would let them know when I would be returning to work. Esther told them the doctors thought that I might have meningitis. When they heard that they sealed off my room till almost the end of the school year. They were afraid of possible contamination. I was not aware that they were doing that until months later. I got a phone call from the principal when I was in the hospital. It was nice to hear from him. I told him of my concern for the students whom I counseled regularly and the students who made up the Busy Buddy Newspaper. I was looking forward to coming back to work and seeing the children again. That was the last time I had any communication with the principal. The secretaries and my co-counselor sent me get well cards but they never visited by phone or in person. I found out many months later that there was a very small notice on the board near the time cards that I was in the hospital. When I had the occasion to call the secretary over half a year after I came home from the hospital, I spoke to one of the faculty members with whom I had a working relationship; he picked up the phone and thought I was transferred to another school. He was unaware that I was sick and had been in the hospital and was no longer able to work. I was hurt that I did not receive any cards from the students, but later found that people did not know what my situation was.

There were many things of which I was not of aware. While in Peninsula Hospital I had two possible strokes. They were shown on the MRIs. The first one showed one lesion. The second had more. It was acute.

I was seen by many different doctors but none of them could give a diagnosis. My speech slowly came back. As the tests came in they found several lesions on my brain. They thought that I would be a good candidate for rehab so they moved me to that section of the hospital. I was moved into the brain trauma unit for rehab and further testing. Still no diagnosis. The doctors had me placed on a strong antiviral medication just in case it was spinal meningitis. The treatment seemed to be working, but still no diagnosis. The doctors agreed that more tests were necessary, but the hospital I was in did not have facilities for the testing I needed. Instead of immediately transferring me to a hospital that could help, they scheduled testing for me at Long Island Jewish Hospital. There was going to be a week wait for them to get me over there for testing. In the interim, they wanted me to continue with the rehab. I had been hospitalized 13 days. I realized they were not helping me with the real problem. I was losing my ability to speak and ambulate. My family found this delay to be unacceptable and had me discharged from Peninsula Hospital.

CHAPTER 3 - New York University Medical Center

I had heard about Rusk Institute/ NYU. After researching, my sister Esther and I went to NYU Hospital. Peninsula hospital did not want to release me. It was difficult dealing with them to get the medical records to which I was entitled. Through my personal doctor's family I could be admitted to NYU Hospital. My sister helped me gather all of my belongings and, in order to avoid the stress of driving, we took a taxi. The cab was a big, older model car. I don't know what make it was. It looked like a wreck. I feared that this would be the last time I would be able to make intelligent communication. I felt my speech and thoughts were on the way out. I thought that my memory might have been also affected. My fear was unfounded. In the bumpy taxi ride there I tried to scribble down notes to Esther. The taxi would have been more pleasant if it had better shock absorbers, but the taxi driver knew the way and made good time on the road and got us there all safe and sound. He pulled up to the emergency room entrance. Esther carried all of my belongings and we went into the emergency admitting room.

The relative of my doctor was waiting for me upon arrival. She was a veteran volunteer and was able to walk me through the admittance process. Before I knew it I was on a bed in the emergency room. Esther was beside me the whole time. Doctors and student doctors were taking information and observing me. In order to make an accurate diagnosis, they decided more tests were needed.

In the interim a doctor (a neurologist specializing in migraines) was brought in. After hearing of my sensitivities to light and noise he decided that all I had was a migraine headache and was going to have me discharged. My sister asked him if he had looked at my

MRI and CAT scans showing the lesions on the brain. He had not. He yelled at us for questioning him and his diagnosis. We immediately asked to have him dismissed and requested to have another doctor. By the way, after an accurate diagnosis from another doctor, he sent me a letter of apology.

One test, an angiogram of the brain, was invasive. It was to be seen by a team of radiologists. It was supposed to take about an hour for this process. Esther waited along with my daughter Mollie. The process continued to go on much longer than expected. Esther was wondering what's taking so long. It was already two and a half hours. Then she overheard the staff talking about someone who had a stroke while on the operating table. That was me. The doctors worked on me over four hours. Thank God that it happened while under their care. The doctors showed Esther and Mollie the pictures of the nerves and vessels affected. They were supposed to look like open straws but they looked like a bunched up shriveled tangled mess.

I had a massive stroke of my left side of the brain, which left speech and the right side of my body impaired. The right side was weaker with a general numbness. My thought processes were intact. My memory was intact. My sense of humor was intact. Because of my inability to communicate with speech I became frustrated and furious. With the analysis of the angiogram and the results from a battery of other tests, a correct diagnosis was made by Dr. Weinberger: **Primary Vasculitis of the Central Nervous System.** It is a rare disease of the immunological system. Vasculitis causing inflammation of the blood vessels to the brain, the symptoms are headache, neck and joint pain, soreness in the temples, numbness of the arms and legs, vision deficit, double vision, and loss of peripheral vision. Dr. Smiles said that this form of vasculitis is so rare that there is not a sufficient group on which to do scientific research. It was the consensus of doctors that with the primary vasculitis of the central nervous system and the massive stroke on top, they didn't have much hope. **They thought if I did survive, I would be a complete vegetable and need constant care.**

CHAPTER 4 - Stroke unit

When a bed was available they moved me to the stroke unit for observation. It was a room with 4 beds; a staff member was to constantly observe. Though it was probably very quiet in the room, everything sounded very loud to me. I couldn't rest. The sound of the staff coming in and out was like thundering rain on a tin rooftop. The sounds of other people in pain who were in the room were also magnified. I couldn't stand it. It was torture.

Dr. Smiles had taken over the major part of my care. He is a rheumatologist. He saw how uncomfortable I was. On the same floor there was a private room available. He arranged for the hospital to give me the room gratis. All I could say was "ahhh."

In the middle of the night I was awakened by two staff members singing happily at the top of their lungs while skipping down the hallway. It sounded like kindergarten recess. If it hadn't been so annoying, I would have thought it very amusing.

Dianna came to stay with me and helped with my care for a week. With the exception of Dianna, I was unable to communicate with speech to other people. Somehow Dianna was able to understand me. Having her small child at home she had the recent experience of deciphering baby talk and translated that into deciphering my attempts at speech. She also was able to take care of my home expenses. In order to find where everything was located I made drawings. These drawings were to indicate locations. To anybody but Dianna and myself, they looked like scribble scrabble, but she was able to understand. She was extremely supportive.

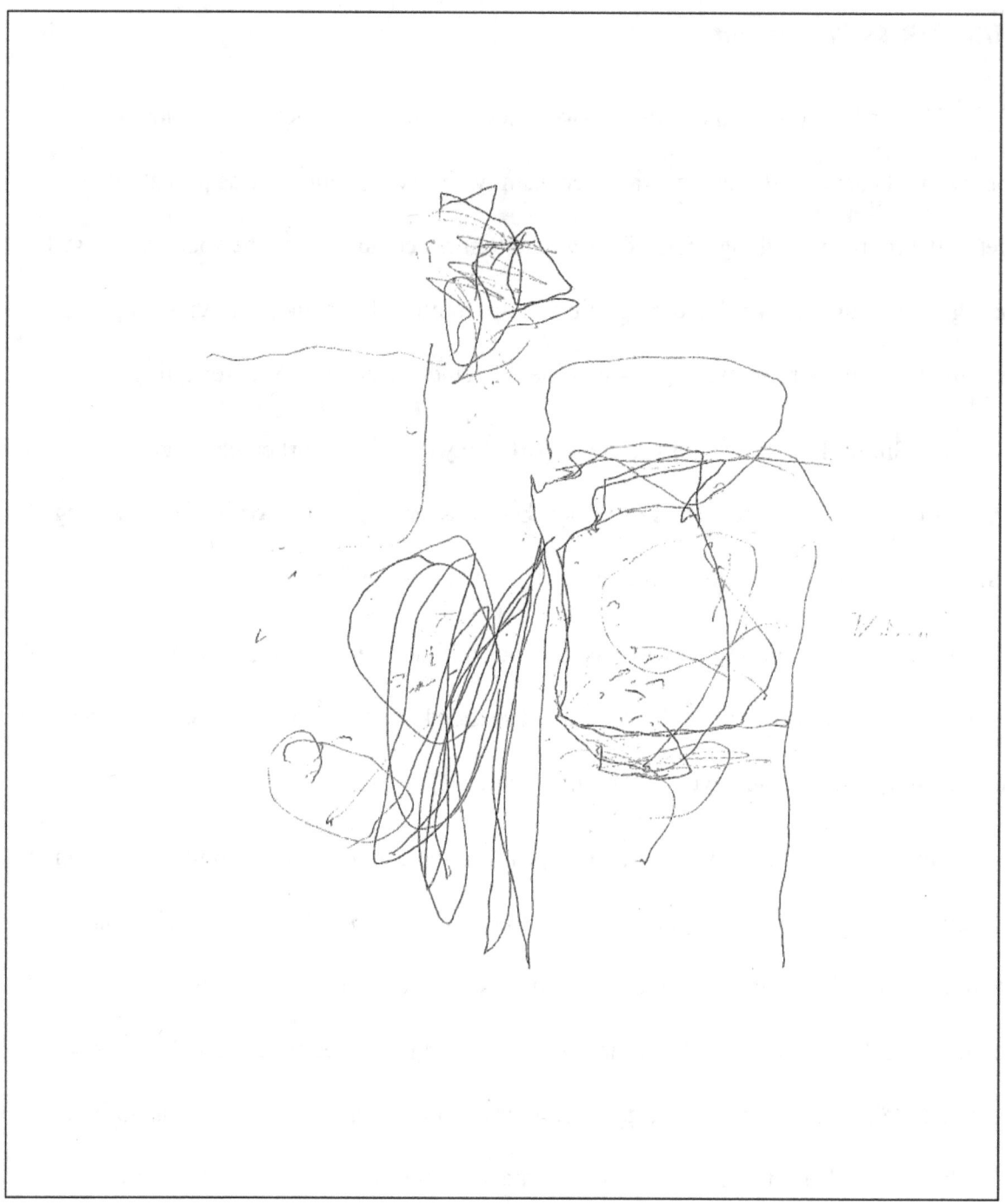

Figure 1: My drawing to show Dianna location of my documents.

My balance was very poor. They wanted me to use the bedpan but I was very uncomfortable and refused. Dianna encouraged me and walked with me while she physically supported me on the way to the bathroom.

Rabbi Chill, the rabbi of my congregation, came to visit me several times during my stay at Tisch Center at NYU. It was very kind of him. I felt sorry for him. He came from Far Rockaway to visit and I could not even speak. It was courageous of him to make a one way conversation. I was so tired, but the visits were uplifting.

Dr. Smiles decided that the best treatment for the vasculitis would be chemotherapy. They don't have a specific treatment yet for vasculitis, so they were using a treatment they thought would parallel conditions that would be used for cancer. With the use of chemo I really had to use the bathroom, but I was very much debilitated (so thank you Dianna).

After a few weeks, Dr. Smiles saw I was well enough to be transferred from Tisch (the main part if the hospital) down stairs to Rusk Rehabilitation Center. I had many doctors involved in my care. They were all professional, but Dr. Smiles I called Smiley, for he really was that, and was very special to me. He really cares. He's a mensch (a real human being). I recognized this in him from the very beginning of our relationship, and I told him I loved him.

CHAPTER 5 - Reactions to medications

I was given many different medications, one of which was steroid (Prednisone). Soon after taking these medications my body changed. I have a very small frame. I wore size 4 and 6 clothing. My hair was full, very curly, and came a little beyond shoulder length. It was dark brown (partially dyed). Now my pajamas no longer fit. Esther went out and brought me new clothing that went from medium to large within one week.

My hair started to thin out. In the course of time it would continually fall out to the point of just covering my head. It fell in handfuls. Clumps of hair would shed into my hand. I would run my wide toothed comb through my hair while taking my shower and see the hair in a pool clogging the drain. The aide was shocked at first. It seemed to be a daily routine till there was so little left that there was just enough to cover my head. When I would comb my hair at the sink trying to make it more presentable it continued to fall out. I was so embarrassed to leave such a mess I tried to clean it with a paper towel before the aides came to help me.

My face became grotesquely swollen. Even though I looked all distorted my features did not make me feel so terrible. They disturbed me but did not throw me over. My sister Esther and all of my children, including my son Eddie who came all the way from Sweden, came to visit. It was a very special Mother's Day with everybody together. Mollie came with her husband Carl and baby Nadiva, Dianna, Michael, Eddie, and Esther.

CHAPTER 6 - Support outside of hospital

Eddie and Michael knew how much energy I had invested in keeping my garden. Taking care of it was a joy for me. There was the lawn and all the plants which I knew mostly by name on the ground floor, and the two porches with flowers, herbs, and vegetables. My two guys helped to maintain it while I was in the hospital. Eddie told me that while they were in the garden, at least twenty friends and neighbors stopped to visit and inquire about my condition. I had no idea that there was such caring. It made me feel so special.

CHAPTER 7 - Rusk Rehabilitation Center: relearning the activities of daily living

I started getting physical therapy. The therapist was to teach me to walk again. Rusk Institute is the part of the hospital for rehabilitation. I was transferred. I was placed in a four-bedded room on the first floor. The nurses and aides were very efficient and focused and well trained in dealing with patients who had a multitude of problems, both physical and the emotional problems that result from illnesses and accidents.

The philosophy at Rusk is: do as much as you are able to do by yourself and they will help you with the rest.

The nurse would give me some rules; take your time, concentrate on one thing at a time, safety first, always wear your feet coverings when out of bed, have assistance getting into and out of the wheelchair.

Eating became an event. I was unable to hold the utensils. I was unable to steady the food on the tray. My right hand was unable to negotiate anything. My entire right side was numb from my toes to the top of my head. I would have to locate my right arm; it could be behind me, in front of me, on the side of me; it had a life of its own. I would wind up dumping the food on the floor. It was very frustrating. The aide would get food replacements and help me. The policy was to do as much as you can, but get assistance when you actually needed it. The goal was to be independent. My right hand is my primary hand. At first I had to learn to use my left hand for everything.

Breakfast was a substantial meal. I wanted to have sufficient calories to be comfortable with the exercise plan, and I was hungry. I started off with a boiled egg, which had to be peeled with assistance. I could not begin my meal without assistance. It was a very important lesson to learn. We need one another. I usually had hot or cold cereal. The package needed to be opened. The container of milk needed to be opened. If I drank with a straw the paper had to be removed. They had very nice challah rolls and dinner rolls, juice, and yogurt, and tea, and I ate it all. I had to save some of the liquid in order to take my pills. There were a whole bunch of pills and I had difficulty swallowing them. Having a bit of food in my mouth made swallowing them easier. Blood tests were taken every day. They showed an imbalance of electrolytes (sodium and potassium), so I was put on fluid restriction. I had to be aware of that part of my diet. I could no longer choose to drink as much as I had been used to.

Every day the menus were given out and had to be filled out with the food choices for the next day's meals. It seemed to be a simple task. The choices were to be circled, unless you wanted a substitution. Holding the pencil was a big chore. I wasn't quite up to the task and writing in alternate choices was beyond my capability. My sister Esther would visit me and fill the menu out. I would usually have a light lunch: a salad, fruit, fruit ices, milk. Milk products became more important to offset the effects of the steroids, which could weaken the bones.

Dinner came in kosher packs. They were heated in the kitchen and served to me very hot. I could not open it myself at all. They were so steaming that it was difficult even for my helpers to take the wrappers off. It was nice to have my meal so nice and hot. There was a variety of food for dinner. I could choose from chicken, pot roast, eggplant parmesan, fish, or turkey, with a vegetable accompaniment. I could choose from a variety of juices, tea, milk, and water. My favorite dessert was the orange ices. I had a challah roll instead of a piece of cake. I had to cut out the challah roll after a while because I realized that it was putting weight on me and it was too easy to become very heavy while taking my medication.

Negotiation of the slippers was humorous. At first the aide would place the slippers on me. When I would reach the bed again the left slipper would drop to the floor but the right slipper insisted on staying on. To this very day it prefers to stay on. A special effort has to be made to remove the right slipper. I would think that my foot was bare in the bed but it was still actually in the slipper.

Washing my hands and face presented different feelings, since the right side of my head was numb.

When going to the toilet I now had to use my left hand to clean myself. Everything was very messy. I could not feel my private parts. I felt unclean and frustrated and everything took so long.

I needed assistance to go from the toilet back to the wheelchair. At times it felt that I had to be patient waiting for the nurse just to move me a few feet to the sink. I was not very successful brushing my teeth. Using the left hand was an entirely different procedure than I was used to. I was unable to feel the right side of my jaw so I was not able to know if I was actually doing it. What a relief when my sister Esther would come to visit me and would brush my teeth for me. Esther came to visit almost every day. She brought me clean laundry and fruit and words of good cheer. She was my mouth. She monitored the progress of the doctors and was able to communicate my needs to them. Esther, Dianna, and Michael broke up various tasks to take care of for me. They took care of hospital, home, and tasks relating to work. **My job was to get healthy.**

I started the rehabilitation at Rusk after an introductory interview where they explained procedures and rules for each discipline.   Two lovely young ladies from the occupational therapy department visited me in my room. They wanted to tell me about occupational therapy and assess my capabilities. They were very cheerful and soft spoken. One of them however needed to have some disciplinary instruction. When she spoke to me she was speaking in a baby voice and speaking as if I was incapable of comprehension. I felt as if I was being spoken to as a child not capable of adult comprehension. My expression changed immediately to anger and without any hesitation I let her know that I was fully capable of understanding her and to please speak to me as an adult. She apologized and we were able to go on from there. This seems to have been a common happening; people want to help when they don't have to, and they think if you are handicapped in any way you must be handicapped in all ways. My son Eddie was with me and enjoying my feisty comeback.

I was given a schedule. My day began with a visit from Dr. Smiles; he's an early bird; a shower, then breakfast, and morning rounds with interns and doctors of various disciplines making their observations (always occurring at breakfast). I would transfer in the wheelchair at 8:45 AM by elevator to the floor where I would begin the physical therapy. From 9:00 AM until 3:30 PM; with a break for lunch; I would have occupational therapy, individual and group speech therapies. The psychologist would see how I was doing also. At 3:30 PM I would go back to physical therapy to get some additional exercise time. It was a full schedule. Every moment that something was not scheduled for me I would take the opportunity to do extra physical or occupational therapy. I wanted to be healthy. I was taken aback when the psychologist wanted to know just how little I would be satisfied with in my recovery. Unfortunately, it is the attitude of some workers in health care disciplines. This negative attitude sets the patient up for less than maximum motivation and self-esteem. Many patients don't have positive reinforcement. With determination, motivation, patience, caring helpers, and of course God's help, one can achieve. I set my record straight. With God's help, I wanted a complete recovery. **I wanted to be healthy.**

CHAPTER 8 - Physical therapy

The physical therapy department was a gym with weights and machines, ramps, a variety of balls, cushions, canes and bars, and places to lie down and exercise, and various other equipment, just like a commercial gym.

The physical therapy program began with individual exercises using machines. One machine would exercise my arms like a bicycle exercises the legs and the other was a leg cycle. Another machine from a sitting position would raise your legs. I walked on a treadmill. There was another machine that helps with balance by using a video screen to indicate the pattern of movement to improve balance. The sessions were a half hour, so I was able to do only some of the exercises each time. After working on the machines I had my individual session with the physical therapist, Peter Walker.

First I was tested on skills to see what my capabilities were at that point. The emphasis was placed on balance. Because my peripheral vision on the right side was gone at that time, I had to be aware and careful negotiating turns. It was as if I had a blinder on my right side. I remember, while practicing walking, I tripped over a waste paper basket and several other objects till I got the hang of turning my head to look over my right shoulder. The therapist worked with me on balance on the ramp and stairs. We also played with different size balls using various techniques. We used the other equipment using a wide range of methods to increase the body's dexterity, strength, and balance.

Physical therapy continued in the afternoon with class work. I walked the long hall for balance. I would try to turn my head from one side to the other and look up and down while going forward. I had to take measured steps, sometimes long, sometimes short or slow to fast. Sometimes we would do dance steps to change directions, extend the legs, and make it interesting. It was called a class but each person was given individual attention and rest when needed, while other patients had their turn. Other skills like coming in and out of a car, entering a tub or shower, the toilet, negotiating a curb and traffic were practiced.

The therapist and I went outside where we put these skills into action. We crossed the streets, looked at the traffic, looked at the holes in the sidewalk, looked to see where we were going, looked for landmarks, and enjoyed getting out of the hospital for our field trip.

The last field trip at Rusk was a culmination of the learning skills that I needed to negotiate in my neighborhood. This time I was accompanied by both the occupational and physical therapists. They sent me on a scavenger hunt. We went several blocks away from the hospital. They gave me a list of things that I was to come back with under their supervision. I had to get my bearings and notice the street signs and my direction. I was given five dollars. I had to find the newspaper store and buy the Post. The fruit store was next. I had to select two grapefruits and bananas and make my speech clear enough for the salesperson to understand my selection. I had to hand over the money and make sure I was getting the right change. The next stop was to locate a mailbox. I walked around and it was a little tricky. We were on very wide streets that had an intermediary street in between. I didn't see it at first and then I realized how could I not have found it? It was right there. I mailed the letter. The next item on the list was a cup of coffee. Starbucks is always around the corner in Manhattan. The restaurants were giving off wonderful smells while getting lunches prepared. We stopped at a pizza and Italian food place for my next item, a slice of pizza. The pizza was to be a reward for me, but the pizzeria wasn't kosher. My two items, the pizza and a take home menu for the occupational and physical therapy staff, completed my list. Now I had to recognize my way back. We had already gone a number of blocks in various directions and it was time for us to have lunch too. I was able to find the way back to the hospital. The scavenger hunt was lots of fun.

CHAPTER 9 - Speech therapy

Speech was next on my program. I began with individual speech therapy. First I was given an introduction, including tests to see my status. My speech was very limited and very unclear, although I knew what I wanted to say. The words would not come out or they would come out with the opposite meaning of what I was trying to say. The speech therapist explained to me that I had apraxia (Total or partial loss of the ability to perform coordinated movements or manipulate objects in the absence of motor or sensory impairment --from dictionary.com) and aphasia (Partial or total loss of the ability to articulate ideas or comprehend spoken or written language, resulting from damage to the brain caused by injury or disease). --from dictionary.com

My response to my difficulties was to laugh when I heard the speech come out of my mouth. It was so funny. As a professional counselor, words were my stock and trade. I was able to use other ways to express myself, including synonyms and gestures. My speech formation at this time was limited at best to words of one syllable. It was pointed out to me that regaining my speech would be a slow process. **The brain in making new pathways cannot be rushed; it has its own time schedule.** Usually the first half of the year is crucial; it's the strongest time of learning and brain pathway formation. The rest of that year is also very important because that's when the pathways are reinforced and augmented. This piece of information was very important to me for my ability to understand and cope with a positive attitude.

My advice to myself is have a positive outlook, focus, relax, respect your ability; it's my responsibility to work as hard as I can towards my recovery, and patience, patience, patience. Take control and direct your brain to do what you want it to do.

Don't put limits on your potential.

I was put into a conversation class with others who had suffered a stroke as I had. At first I was afraid to open my mouth. My voice sounded strained and strange. The pitch was high and screeching. The intonation was foreign. I spoke without prepositions and other small connecting words as if English was my second language. A patient from France thought I was also from France. When I heard one of the doctors from Hungary speak, I recognized the accent and intonation as my own. I had no control of the new mode of speech. Interestingly, my maternal grandmother was from Hungary, although I had little contact with her as she was ill and died just before I was three. Trying to converse in the class gave me confidence to try to express myself. I saw and understood the struggle my classmates were having. We tried to express our feelings and during the course of conversation we would tell our past and present experiences. One person loved to travel all over the world; another was very involved with family and loved to cook. Along with those positives we were sensing the loss of our ability to communicate as we had. It was easy to see my classmates' loss of self-esteem. I was determined not to let that happen to me.

Individual speech therapy gave me strength for strategies; asking yes and no questions, giving three word verbal choices, completing a sentence, i.e. fill in the blank, using distraction free environment, and better (more suitable) informal tasks. We went over everyday words, the numbers, the weeks, months, and time; words having to do with the basic needs, i.e. light, telephone, hungry, hot and cold. We looked at emotion words i.e. happy, sad, frustrated, angry, tired, fine, and healthy. We tried to introduce as many concepts as we could through the course of speech while talking about areas of interest to me.

Every night I would speak with Michael for half an hour to an hour to specifically work on speech. My speech therapist said that this is one of the best ways to improve and people would tell me my speech improved every week and it still is improving.

In addition to speaking, my speech therapist, Karen Gendal, gave me written homework for writing and for reading. One of the techniques she used when I could not pronounce the words was to have us sing it and I was able to do it. She had a good voice.

One of the things brought to me at Peninsula Hospital was my siddur, a prayer book which I had been using on a daily basis and wished that I could still use. When Esther gathered my things together to go to NYU she left most of my things at home, including my siddur. At the beginning I was in no condition to use it, though I spoke to God all the time.

When I went to Rusk I spoke with the rabbi and asked him to bring me a siddur with large print. At first I could not read any part at all, even with the large print. Then I could discern the shapes of the letters and as I practiced I was able with much patience to say a little bit of the prayers. One that I especially liked at the beginning of the prayer book was in the morning prayers: "How precious is your kindness, Oh God! The sons of man take refuge in the shadows of your wings. May they be sated from the abundance of Your house; and may You give them to drink from the stream of Your delights. For with you is the source of life--by Your light we shall see light. Extend Your kindness to those who know You and Your charity to the upright of heart." (From the Artscroll Siddur, August 1994 edition, page 5) As I was able to write, I wrote this translation out for my speech therapist and she was so impressed with my writing and enjoyed the prayer so much that I gave it to her and she framed it.

CHAPTER 10 - Occupational therapy

In occupational therapy we worked on speech, but not in the same way as speech therapy. I practiced writing the forms of the letters, learning to use my hands with the Palmer Method, making circles and diagonals. I was applying both hands to write. Now I'm able to use my dominant right hand again, though it still had no feeling. They gave me exercises where I would circle words that belong to the same category and I would follow the same type of thinking in speech and try to pronounce the words. There were many exercises to increase the mobility and flexibility of my hand and arm. I used a material like silly putty. Another exercise used was, a container of rice containing a variety of materials such as coins, buttons, and beads. I would try to separate them while feeling the different textures. We worked on closing and opening buttons. One of the most difficult skills they taught me was to use a scissors. I found that planning was enormously difficult for me, especially with the apraxia. I had to constantly refer to my left hand to hold and to coordinate the scissors with my right hand. The task was almost impossible. I spent much time trying to learn this skill.

I had a lot of fun working with some of the therapists who had a background in dance. I had been dancing since my childhood. I love to dance and when I was in the beginning of high school we were given aptitude tests, I was to teach dance. How right it was. I started teaching dance when I was sixteen to a group of teenagers and I have been doing that on and off ever since. The physical therapist and I worked on doing bar exercises and dance combinations calling for center work. First working the combination on one side then on the other, planning and performing the movements was very challenging but great fun. The occupational therapist was formerly a dancer with one of the New York City ballet companies. She helped me make it fun by stretching my mind and body as well. It's wonderful how the therapists were able to combine their skills and my interests.

While enjoying the exercise of finger painting some spilled on my new yellow outfit. I went back to my room and changed. And brought the pants back to the physical therapy room where I tried to clean the paint from the pants. The stains just were not budging. The whole thing was an exercise for my hands; the squeezing, pushing, turning motions were very therapeutic, although frustrating not being able to erase the stains.

Nettie Capasso, my therapist, brought from her home a cleanser (Oxi-Clean) that we tried the next day that worked much better, not perfect but much better. We tried one more way; we went to the area in another part of the building where they had a kitchen, living room, dining room, and laundry setup. This was an opportunity to independently use the skills learned using the washer and dryer under the supervision of Nettie. Success!

On the third floor there was a replica of a kitchen where I was prepared to use many skills of daily living. I needed to look at spice containers, move them and put them in different orders. My arm muscles were very weak and it was very difficult to coordinate opening the refrigerator door. Eventually I was able to do this and lift out a quart container of juice. These tasks that we take for granted became wonderful accomplishments.

Bending down to access the pots and pans in the cabinets, I had to use my flexibility and

To Squat, feet are planted on the floor. Knees do not go past the toes. The torso may lean forward, making it easier to rise. Squats are used to sit and rise.

my balance and learn to squat.

I fell many times learning to do this. The most difficult part was to get up from the floor. It was very difficult because there was no feeling on the right side. The muscles on the right side were working but the nerves sending the messages of sensation were not. I was able to walk because, somehow, even without visual input, the left side was able to coordinate the movements of the right to produce walking. Dr. Smiles, nine years later, said that the neurologists are without an answer for this process. While relearning to wash dishes, the same kind of conversation takes place in my brain between the left and unfeeling right hand where the motions are compensated for by the feeling hand. Interestingly, the signals have to do with place; the hands seem to be coordinated in the task when they are in front of me; when the right hand moves to the side or behind, the right hand is not aware of the new placement and reacts as though it were still in the front. My arm seemed to be playing a game of hide and seek.

No feeling on the right side had its advantages. Blood was drawn every morning and I felt no pain when it was taken from that side. The disadvantages were that I had to be very careful recognizing the right temperature for my right side. This was very important to do, especially when I was taking a shower.

I needed heightened awareness of my surroundings, especially when using knives, using the stove to cook, and placing pots on the stove. I attempted to make a can of soup but found that I was unable to open the can. That would come in time many months later.

My activities of daily living included dressing myself. I was soon able to do this without assistance, with the exception of tying my shoes. My son Michael and I would visit in the relaxed setting of the hospital garden, where he taught me to tie my shoelaces again. It took a lot of concentration and patience for myself, as well as for Michael. I spent much time practicing this skill. By the time I was discharged from the hospital I was able to do it.

CHAPTER 11 - Extracurricular activities

Some of the activities that were not part of the daily routine during the evening were cooking and music. We gathered together for a sing along, accompanied by the guitar. We had lyric sheets and we would choose from many selections. At first I could not decipher the print. I could not tell if the sheet was upside down. It all looked like hieroglyphics to me. My speech was so poor I could not sing along with the group, but I knew this would help me with my speech, and it was enjoyable just to be in a social setting. As the weeks progressed I was able to distinguish the words and sing some of the songs. We were enjoying it so much that it seemed the sessions were never long enough. It was a very bright moment for me that my sister Esther was able to share this activity with me several times.

Cooking was always fun. The leader would pass out a recipe and we would go over the details. We would gather the materials necessary for the recipe and work on measuring ingredients and putting them all together to form dough for cookies. While the cookies baked we had time to socialize, which gave me further opportunity to work on my speech.

During Eddie's visits he was also impressed with the results of all my therapies. I was able to count up to four while lifting a small weight. He and my daughter-in-law, Catherine, could see improvement in my ability to plan. I was able to negotiate my balance and direction, always being aware of my lack of peripheral vision on my right side, as I held the banister and climbed up and down the stairs. It was a lot of physical and mental coordination. There was always the stress of focusing. One technique I had used was rap music, which had I composed to teach students key points; now I used on myself. Specifically: Do what you do, when you're doing it.

CHAPTER 12 - TISCH

A month had gone by since I had the chemotherapy treatment at Tisch.

The treatment was tentatively scheduled for once a month. Dr. Smiles, my rheumatologist, unfortunately became ill and it was postponed till he would be able to supervise my treatment. During this time I also became ill. I suffered a major reaction to the buildup of medications. I had fever and my body was more blown up than it already had been. I was covered from head to toe with a rash. My face was like a ripe pumpkin. They stopped every medication that was not absolutely necessary. I was transferred back over to Tisch, the main part of NYU Hospital. The insurance coverage at Rusk had come to an end. I was greatly disappointed that I was unable to continue the remedial treatment, which had been so valuable to me during my stay there. However, I had to move on and be treated for the skin condition and the possible effects on my liver. While at Tisch they biopsied my skin and kept watch on my liver through my blood. They did not know exactly what part of my body could be affected by all this. My body was doused with creams and lotions. I rested quite a bit and felt strong again, although my rash was still prevalent I was getting much stronger. I soon was able to exercise on my own. I was able to walk to the shower room without the wheelchair and shower without assistance and/or supervision. The key to walking with poise and without pain is good posture.

I was able to walk the long corridor. I made a track for myself. The floor was rectangular in its shape with rooms on the perimeter and nurses' station in the center; other rooms, offices, and nursing stations divided the center. I speed walked in one direction and

> **Posture** is controlled by the core muscles - the abdominal muscles and the erector spinae lower back muscles (the muscles just above your buttocks, on either side of your spine).

then followed in the other for 20 minutes, which I calculated to be one mile. I came through like a steamroller. I was tired but invigorated and able to rest after that. I used the handrails in the corridor like a dance bar for exercise to practice balancing my legs, changing levels and directions and stretching my arms and legs. I wanted to retain the progress that I had made so far.

> **Exercise the Feet** while sitting or standing:
>
> Squeeze the feet, arching the foot. Release.
> Repeat 3 times
>
> Squeeze the feet, making fists with the feet. Release.
> Repeat 3 times
>
> Lift the left heel. Ball of the foot rests on the floor. Release.
> Lift the right heel. Ball of the foot rests on the floor. Release.
> Alternate repeating 3 times
>
> Lift the left heel, roll the ball of the foot until the tip of the toes rests on the floor. Reverse. Lower the toes to the ball, and then the heel.
> Repeat on the right foot.
> Alternate repeating 3 times.

CHAPTER 13 - Another rehab facility

It was time to make new arrangements for my care. My rash had greatly subsided. The doctors could see no further use for my hospital stay. My visit in the hospital was no longer covered by the insurance. The option was to go to another rehab facility or go home. My family wanted very much to extend my care in the rehab facility. This was not my first choice. But they were very insistent and I thought perhaps they had my best interests at heart. After looking at the facilities that were available, a choice was made. All the documents were prepared for the transfer and on June 30, '05, I packed my belongings, said my goodbyes, and Esther drove me to the rehab facility where we were expected.

The facility was basically a nursing home with a rehab component. From my past experience working in nursing homes, and with one of my relatives being in a nursing home, I knew that this was not the place I would ever prefer to be. But I knew that there might be some value to my recuperation. I was told that the length of my stay would be up to me, depending how beneficial I found it to be. I had the option to stay as long as a month or as little as a few days. Esther and I were shown the room. It was nice enough. It was a two-bedded room with two televisions. I noticed the woman who I would be sharing the room with was enjoying her television at high volume. Esther and I spoke with the staff to find out about using headphones so that each person could enjoy hearing television in privacy. When I was in the hospital the use of headphones for television or any sound equipment was standard. I personally preferred not to have the use of television. I found the light very difficult on my eyes and the sound annoying and at times unbearable. The staff was unable to accommodate my needs. Without further ado, we left.

As we were already in Brooklyn, Esther drove us to her home. I thought we were going to go back to my home but we wound up staying overnight with her in Brooklyn. Her thought was to keep me there a few days, at least to observe how I would do, but that was not my idea. The following day she brought me home.

CHAPTER 14 – Home

How good it was to be home again.

I had been away from April 23 to July 1. I found myself walking up the stairs to the second floor where I lived. Using the skills that I had learned, I was confident that I would continue to improve. Esther stayed with me that day and helped me to get settled in. When in Brooklyn she had already helped me get my prescriptions filled. And on the way we stopped in the kosher supermarket and selected a variety of takeout foods to take home. Esther stayed until the evening, when my son Michael arrived to stay with me. He took off work and stayed with me a week to see that I was able to care for myself.

The therapist told me I might be frustrated because of the time it would take to do a task when by myself and that I might find myself getting tired. Michael was very understanding. He gave me time to rest as well as time to try to do as much as I could. The laundry area is in the basement and my living area is on the second floor, so I still needed help bringing my laundry up and down the steps.

Cooking: I was able to use food that did not need to be cooked, only cold food or that which could be microwaved. I was afraid to use the stove on my own. I wasn't sure about holding things. I felt it was unsafe. I was for sure unable to use the igniter for the stove and oven. Six months later I was able to do it. At first I couldn't use a vegetable peeler. I discovered cleaned, fresh baby carrots. I washed my vegetables very carefully.

> **Focus.** If you lose your focus, take a breath, a long, full, deep breath or two to help relieve stress and energize your cognition to stay on task.

Knives were very dangerous in my hands. It was important to have things uncluttered so I could get things without hurting myself. Michael separated knives so I could have easy access. He oversaw my use of the knives and reminded me to **focus** on the project. Anytime I did not concentrate I cut myself. This could be dangerous even with a small cut, because with the medication I am taking it takes too long for the blood to stop flowing.

Soon after I arrived home, my neighbors noticed that I was here. One of my neighbors came knocking on my door to welcome me back and visit me with fresh baked potato kugel. My neighbors and friends in the community were and still are very supportive. From the time this sickness came about, the entire community said prayers for me on a daily basis, for which I am forever grateful.

Michael took the week off from work to take care of me but he did have to go back to work. He came every Sunday to visit and help me in any way that I needed and calls me every day.

I had visitors from my community from the time I went to the hospital. They told me that prayers were said for me individually and by the whole community on a daily basis. God has been answering their prayers as evidenced by my great and continuing improvement. There are many ways that people help. Hatzala is the volunteer communal ambulance department that brought me to the hospital. Members of the Bikur Cholim, an organization helping the Jewish community, acted on my behalf. It is all voluntary. People would make visits to the sick at the hospital. They would bring electric candles to observe the Sabbath. When I needed to get to the doctors and I did not have transportation, people picked me up and brought me to my appointments. When I was out of the hospital they brought me home cooked food from different members of the community. People would drive up to my home and deliver it hot and it was delicious. They helped me with the food for an extended period of time, which was greatly appreciated. I am thankful that I am just starting to be able to cook regular meals for myself. There are so many ways that people can repay kindness. I am looking forward to being able to do that.

CHAPTER 15 - Using a telephone

How would we exist without the telephone? From the beginning in Peninsula Hospital I was able to communicate by phone before my speech was severely affected by the massive stroke. At NYU, although I was unable to speak after the stroke, I was still insistent to have the telephone turned on. It was a source of comfort to know that I could be connected to the outside world. It sounds silly, especially since I couldn't even reach the phone. It did get some use when Esther or Dianna needed to call out. When I was transferred to Rusk I was again connected to the phone. At this point I was able to hold the receiver with my left hand when someone called me. Of course my speech was so poor that nobody could understand me on the telephone. My family members and very close friends were the people who called me and knew that was the case.

It was very difficult to use the hospital's phone system. On this system you have to be very fast. You have to first dial the appropriate numbers to reach the outside line and then of course the area code and all the numbers to follow. If there is any delay in the dialing process the system does not allow you to complete the call. I cannot tell you how frustrating this can be, even if you are perfectly healthy and want to dial out, to be cut off when you can't remember the rest of the numbers fast enough. How much more difficult and stressful and frustrating is it when you have an impediment. I thought often how, the system could be improved for the type of client using this facility. I knew I had to work on this skill, together with working on numbers and seeing them in order. I asked for help through the occupational therapy and speech therapy departments. I tried to learn to write and to recognize the numbers' order. I tried to copy them in different order as though they were telephone numbers. I tried to use my fingers to count the numbers. I was so proud when I could get up to five, and then to ten. I separated a deck of cards, which was an enormous exercise in itself, so that I could handle and visualize a suit of numbers and put them in order. Then I would also put them together and say them randomly. I would copy my telephone number and attempt to dial it, using the push buttons under the speech teacher's supervision. I made many attempts; one was successful, though when I continued I wasn't able to complete the call. It was mostly hit or miss. When I was by myself in my room I continued to try on my own. It was very discouraging. It was easier for me to get help from the staff and people who were visiting other roommates. By the time I came home I was more comfortable with recognizing numbers and it was a relief not to have the hospital calling system to deal with. However, I was still unable to use the phone the way I had in the past. What a wonderful thing is this new technology. Esther went shopping and among the many things she purchased was a cordless telephone that could be programmed.

Michael connected everything. There were two phones in the set along with the answering machine. He programmed the most important numbers: his, Esther's, the ambulance, all my children; Dianna, Eddie, Mollie, Dr. Smiles, and some friends. Now I had to learn how to access all of this. How did I do it? **I had to break the task into individual steps**. First I had to press the top left button; then the one on the right, and then I had to decide if I needed the up or down arrow key and press that one to scroll to my selection, and then I could press the on key to complete the calling process. When my call was completed I had to remind myself to press the off key or else I would get the annoying reminder message. Eventually I learned to use the redial, the previous call list, and the answering machine. I'm sure that there are more functions that I'm not aware of yet. One really neat thing about this phone is that I can dial the numbers and see them on the screen before putting the call through. This is very helpful now that I can make calls that are not preprogrammed; I can see my mistakes and use the backspace button to correct the error.

CHAPTER 16 - Visiting nurse services: physical, occupational, and speech therapy and an aide

The visiting nurse service is a private organization that offers different types of home care. Esther got in touch with them to make an appointment to evaluate my needs. They sent someone to give me physical and occupational therapy. I thought that they would do much more. The level of therapy was very basic compared to what had already been taught to me at Rusk.

Exercise: Hold your body erect. **Focus** on a point at eye level to aid your balance. <u>Do the following 2 exercises (standing) first with feet straight ahead and then feet out (toes facing away from the body)</u>.

1. Extend the leg with the straight knee to the front.
   Extend the leg with the straight knee to the back.
   Swing leg back and forth like a pendulum 4 times.
   Change leg and repeat exercise.

2. Extend the leg with the straight knee to the side.
   Repeat 3 times
   Change leg and repeat exercise

I was very disappointed with the therapy. I was given not more than two weeks of therapy. I was terminated because I was able to walk independently and they considered me not housebound, even though I could not really get around outside of my house. They were very limited in their use of equipment, **using a kitchen counter** for balance, which is not bad but was the only exercise the physical therapist gave me.

I live on the second floor of my house and the laundry room is in the basement. The first landing has five steps to enter the house from the outside.

> **Exercise** to strengthen the glutei and thigh muscles to mount **steps**.
> Hold the banister. Look ahead.
> Using the glutei and thigh muscles, alternating legs lift the legs as if marching.
> Repeat 3 times
> Lift legs knee height.
> Repeat 3 times

There are sixteen steps to the second floor. One of the jobs of the therapist is to see that I can do daily chores such as laundry. There are thirteen steps down to the laundry. How am I going to get both myself and the laundry down both flights of stairs?

> **Knee bends** are useful to pick up an object from the ground without straining your back.
>
> Stand in a comfortable wide open stance. Using the abdomen, gluteus muscles, thighs, and calf muscles, bend the knees. Note: In performing knee bends, the heels are directly in line with the buttocks. Take a deep breath. Pick up the object and stand up.

Normally I would carry the laundry basket in one hand and support myself on the banister with the other hand. My arms were not as strong as they were before the illness and my right side was still without the proper nerve feeling. Instead of the basket, I put the laundry into a pillowcase, made a smaller bundle, and threw it down the steps, when I

had to **pick it up** at the first landing. Then I carried it to the second landing, where I threw it to the basement. The basement steps are extra narrow and care had to be taken. I already was comfortable using my washer and dryer. The occupational therapist agreed with me that **folding my clothes** was excellent therapy. It uses the movements of the shoulders, arms, wrists, and fingers.

Exercise for shoulder, elbow, arm, wrist, and fingers

Place arms down at sides. Inhale.
   In sequence, lift left shoulder up (to the left side of the body), lift elbow, with arm extended straight up, lift wrist, and last up hand. (Like a flower unfolding)
   Turn hand palm down. Exhale, slowly saying the word PRESS as you lower your hand to the side and lift heels from the floor.
  Hold the balance. Gently lower your heels. Repeat on right side.
     Note: Saying the word PRESS out loud forces the abdomen to engage and help to keep the balance while elevating.

Open all the fingers. Spread the fingers as though you would palm a basketball. Close them. Repeat several times.

One by one, the thumb touches the tip of each finger.   Repeat.
Shake hand to release tension.

Now to get the clothes back upstairs was another story. As much as I tried the task,

I couldn't do it.

The physical therapist did not see that this was a problem. He showed a lack of empathy. He had no understanding of what was involved in my problem, or as a matter of fact, any person with this problem. This demonstrates how people in the therapy field don't have the internalized experience to really understand the disability. I solved the problem by having my son carry the laundry. The occupational therapist recommended that the best therapy I could do involved daily living experiences. When the bed linens were washed and brought upstairs he said, **"Make your bed."** I have a king size bed. Under normal circumstances it takes a little effort to put all this together. The planning was very important. I had to work with my apraxia to plan out how to accomplish this task and then physically to do it. It involved **stretching my arms in many different ways, balance, bending, and coordination of hands and fingers to pull the sheets over the corners of the bed.**

> **Exercise** to strengthen and increase flexibility of back and arms
>
> Picture yourself rowing. Sit tall either on chair or on floor.
> Pick up your oars at your sides. Hold the oars and sit tall with a flat back.
> Extend the arms and reach forward. Lower the oars into the water.
> Pull the oars back through the water while contracting the back.
> Lift the oars out from the water.
> Repeat.
>
> With palms down, turn hands from the wrists making circles to the left, then to the right.
> With palms up, turn hands from the wrists making circles to the left, then to the right.

The occupational therapist who had been working with me at Rusk had been trying to teach me to use a scissors. I asked the new occupational therapist to continue to do work with this skill but he said it was too difficult for me and refused to help me. I became angry and disappointed. I was not going to give up. Because of the limitation of insurance coverage and of the therapists themselves, that part of the therapy discontinued. I would have to do it on my own.

The speech therapist was called in by the visiting nurses to evaluate my speech. There again, it was terminated by the insurance company before it began, due to my ability to walk. It certainly made no sense to me, the relationship between walking and speech therapy. During the second week they sent me a home health aide to help with household chores. She was a very nice lady who initially took her time about accomplishing her chores, but she soon became efficient. She started slowly but became efficient in her own way. She assisted in rearranging my pantry closet. It was a very big job. She was very bright and cheerful while doing this task. It took more than two days to accomplish this task. Everything was cleared out, cleaned, rearranged in order, and replaced. By the end of the third day she was terminated also. The closet was still not finished. The home health aide felt very bad about the visiting nurses terminating the service, so she volunteered on her own to come to help me. It was such a kindness. She really touched my heart with her consideration and her values.

CHAPTER 17 - Medical tests

The doctor prescribed blood tests every week to check my progress, make arrangements for the chemo therapy treatments, and see that there would be no interference from the medications. Quest Diagnostics sent the hematologist, Maria. Maria contacted Esther every week to remind me of the appointment, since my speech was still not good enough to be contacted by phone. Every Thursday morning she took samples of my blood. She was very efficient, pleasant, and she did not hurt me.

Dr. Smiles received the reports and mailed back a copy of them with his comments. My liver was a big concern, which was one of the things that were showing up on the blood results. At first Dr. Smiles had me coming to him for checkups frequently. He sent me for various tests along the road, MRI, etc. When the blood was not making the progress that was expected Dr. Smiles sent me for a liver biopsy. This was to take place at NYU in the outpatient part of the hospital. I was scheduled to be there at 6:30 in the morning. The Bikur Cholim tried to arrange a volunteer to bring me to the hospital but it was too early for the people who go to work to get there so the Bikur Cholim hired a cab which took me from my home to the hospital, where I was to meet Esther. I was not sure where in the hospital I was to go. I was directed to one area where the receptionist said to wait. After waiting a considerable time it was found that this was not the place and was redirected. The next area I went to was the same story; I had to wait again. After waiting around and getting very concerned that I was missing my appointment, they found out where I actually should be and they gave me a snappy come back, "don't worry; the doctor won't start without you." I found where Esther was. She had been patiently waiting for me. I was given a bed to stay in and the doctor was there.

Dr. Smiles referred me to a specialist to confirm his diagnosis. The specialist prepared me for the liver biopsy telling me in his office that it would involve a certain amount of pain, that it would feel as though I would be kicked in the stomach. The procedure was done in the hospital with a local anesthetic. The procedure itself did not take very long; the preparation took much longer than the procedure itself. The doctor was sure of hand and his warning of pain prepared me so that it seemed small. When he removed the tissue section for the biopsy he admired the healthy tissue and showed it to me. He instructed me that I had to lie on my side for the next several hours to heal so that the blood would not flow from the wound. Esther is disturbed by medical paraphernalia, so during the operation she waited outside. When she came back into the room the doctor offered to show her the tissue and she almost fainted and got horrified and told him she preferred not. So I lay on my side and rested while the nurse was stationed in my room to observe me. Esther stayed by my side for quite a while, then took a walk and came back intermittently to see if I was awake and needed anything. I slept almost the whole day. By evening, around 5pm, I was ready to leave. Esther drove me home. Dr. Smiles was very happy to hear the good news about the biopsy.

CHAPTER 18 – Swimming

The summer was beautiful. In the years past I would take advantage of wonderful warm weather and walk to the beach, which is six tenths of a mile from my house, and go swimming. I live in Far Rockaway. There is a channel leading out to the ocean; except for slack tide when the waters are calm, the current becomes very strong and it is extremely difficult to swim in any way but with the current. However, it's lots of fun to ride the current. I would meet with Russian friends whom I have gotten to know over the years. We would swim together from 7 o'clock in the morning until 8 or 9 AM, when it was too hot to be in the sun already and people would have to go to work or whatever their plans were for the day. They would exercise on the shore and we would socialize while swimming. We would swim a distance and then walk back so that we could ride the current to do it again. As soon as I felt strong enough to walk to the beach, I started my old familiar routine again. **Walking entailed using new skills or being aware of the skills needed.** I walked much slower. I had to be very aware of the lay of the land, the cracks in the sidewalk, gates that may be open in my way, driveways that slope, curbs, depressions in the road, and any other obstacles around. I first put on a pair of beach slippers to walk and that was unsatisfactory. I had difficulty with balance, and due to not feeling my right leg I was unable to keep the slipper on my foot. I would go a few steps and discover I didn't have the slipper on anymore; it was a few steps behind me. I had to backtrack and put it on. Needless to say I changed my footwear. From then on I wore sneakers. They were comfortable, they gave me some support, and they stayed on my feet.

Swimming was natural to me, but I was of course not feeling my right side as I had in the past. I stayed very close to the shore. My friends were very considerate of my situation.

They stayed with me. I swam more slowly than I had in the past. The exercise of swimming was never to be part of a race, but to exercise, socialize, and even meditate while in the water. This was a very invigorating way to start my day. My swim routine consisted of alternating several strokes: crawl, back stroke, side stroke (left and right), breast stroke (front and back). When I'm not able to use the ocean or a pool, I stretch my arms and legs using swim strokes while sitting or walking or lying down.

The beach offers me solace. When I come in the morning there is freshness of air and of spirit. The sun is waking up, the pigeons and sea gulls gather, the 12 swans add to the beauty. Fishermen line the beach while the gentle waves lap the shore. The sand was surrounded by dunes on one side, and jetties on the other. My footprints left sculptures in the sand to be washed away by the wind and the tides.

CHAPTER 19 - Meals and meds

The day actually started with my medications, which had to be taken 5 times a day with the exception of six times a day one day a week. I would first take the medication and then have my morning prayers and be off to the beach for my swim. When I returned I would rinse my bathing suit and take a refreshing cold shower, and then prepare my breakfast, which usually consisted of oatmeal or cold cereal or yogurt or egg, or combinations of those. Breakfast was very important because I had to take several medications with food. Lunch was my next big meal, which was taken without medication. Then midway between waking and going to sleep was the third medication, which had to be taken two hours before eating and two hours after eating. Dinner had to be taken with medication and finally before sleeping medication had to be without eating for two hours. I had to regulate my diet to conform to the medication. I found that it was a cruel taskmaster. It became easier to skip lunch. I got used to this pattern and found that I needed only two very good meals a day. At times I needed only a piece of fruit in between for a snack or some fresh apple or carrot juice from the juicer. I was able to control my weight gain as well by doing this. The medication gives you an appetite so staying at my present weight was quite a feat. I had to work very hard to get control of myself when we celebrated Thanksgiving.

CHAPTER 20 - Dressing myself

Buttoning and zipping: Trying to use two hands with one numb arm was a challenge. Usually I dressed with pullovers and elasticized pants. On Shabbat (Sabbath) I would dress up. Esther took me shopping and got me beautiful outfits. Nothing that I already, had fit. I chose the style that had a series of tiny buttons. I didn't realize what I was in for. When I had been at Rusk they gave me an exercise to learn to open and close buttons, but they used very big buttons. Size matters! Making small, precise movements are very difficult. It's **hard to grasp tiny things,** especially when you don't have the input of sensation. It takes a long time to get dressed. I did find a way to cheat by leaving some of the buttons buttoned and pulling the sweater over my head. That presented another problem. My right arm had to find a way to locate the sleeve to put it on. In any case, I used both methods to get dressed.

Using zippers was not so bad when closing my skirts. It was only rarely bad, when

---

Exercises I used for flexibility and strength of the hands.

Exercise A

1. Make a fist.
2. Open the thumb and stretch it away your palm. Keep it open.
3. Open the index finger and stretch it away your palm. Keep it open.
4. Open the tall finger and stretch it away your palm. Keep it open.
5. Open the ring finger and stretch it away your palm. Keep it open.
6. Open the pinky finger and stretch it away your palm. Keep it open.
   Reverse.
   Return to the fist position by fingers one by one. Close the thumb, index, tall finger, ring finger, and pinky.
   Now start the exercise by opening the pinky, ring finger, tall finger, index finger, and thumb.
   Bring each finger back to the fist.
   Start with pinky then ring, tall, index, lastly, thumb.
   Repeat on other hand.

Exercise B

7. Pretend you are going to make grapefruit juice. Hold the grapefruit in your palm with your fingers clutching the grapefruit. Squeezzzze.

Repeat with the other hand.

the zipper got caught. It was different however when the weather changed and I put on my jacket. The zipper of the jacket was constructed with two tabs. Both tabs had to be held at the same time while placing them into the opposing teeth. The zipper had to be held in the exact angle to work properly with the right amount of space between the two tabs. Sometimes it worked so well; the others, well you can imagine. Many times I thought I was ready to leave the house, only to find that I had to fuss around with the zipper and finally do it.

By the time I got downstairs to my front door I was ready to take out my key and fasten the door, but it was not so simple. I was used to closing the door with my right hand, which now lacked sensation and was unable to do it. The procedure is very different coming from the left side. It took a great deal of thinking to plan the actions. Each movement had to be recalculated. It was as though I was fighting myself when I wanted to turn my hand. It wanted to go in one direction instead of the other. I would try to just pull out the key and could not even get that right. I wound up looking for neighbors to help me. Sometimes I had to wait till somebody was coming around. Practice is the way! I finally made it, but it's still not perfect.

CHAPTER 21 - Stress

At Rusk I was seen by the psychiatrist. He was concerned by my moods. To me my moods were fine. I had a healthy attitude. He was concerned that nothing would endanger that. He put me on an antidepressant to insure a positive state of mind. He checked up on me and within 1 week the dosage was lowered and finally removed after 2 weeks.

The psychologist was also looking after my psychological well-being. My attitude was generally healthy. She was not concerned that I would occasionally feel down on myself. My typical attitude was hopeful, positive, and with faith in God that everything would be done in the right way. My attitude continues to stay positive but, now that I am able to do so much for myself, there is a great deal of added stress.

Work to improve the house, which had started before my illness, was continuing; I had to deal with workers, architects, and the building department to obtain a certificate of occupancy. I had to be very lucky to find workers who were responsible and reliable. The architect and building department all had their own time schedule. I used to think that I was a very patient person. I came to realize in the last few years that my patience could always be improved.

With Michael I was able to work on the bills. I was able to take more responsibility for my finances. There were times I could even write out a check, which takes not only fine motor skills, but also cognitive organization.

And then there was the process of going for Social Security Disability Insurance. The stress of all the paperwork and physical examination also wears one down. Thank God that with Esther's help it has taken place.

I had to deal with financial matters having to do with my pension and all the red tape that it entails and am still dealing with it. Esther was instrumental in helping me deal with this. Now I am doing it pretty much on my own. I still want her support but I am trying to work it out on my own. You can wait months without receiving any finance from the pension. It can certainly put your mood into a very depressed state when you have nothing left and all you can do is borrow and wonder how you are going to be able to pay it back.

CHAPTER 22 - Reducing medications

I've been taking the same medications since I came home from the hospital; that's six months. I was using my local pharmacy initially. My insurance coverage called for using their mail order pharmacy when the prescription total goes over a certain amount and is continually renewed. I reached that point and received my three months' allotment. While taking the prescriptions I noticed that I did not have sufficient tablets of prednisone. My prescription was to take two 5 mg tablets twice a day. At this point I saw only 40 tablets left where there was supposed to have been about two months' worth. Ten days was not sufficient time to have the prescription reordered and sent back to me. I spoke to the customer service person. He was very polite and advised me that if there was a mistake on the prescription they would take care of it and would send it by priority mail. However, if it was correct, I would have to get another prescription from my doctor and have the missing amount filled by another pharmacy. I called my doctor. The receptionist was now aware of my needs and I requested to speak to the doctor when he was finished with his patients.

I wanted to find out if the doctor had actually wanted me to have the prescription decreased to just 2 mg, twice a day. I was anxious to hear from him but could not wait any longer that afternoon since I had an appointment with the dentist. When I returned I had a message on my answering machine from Dr. Smiles telling me that he would like me to have the amount decreased. I was pleased to hear that the steroid had been decreased and he said to call the following morning. So I did. The receptionist gave the message to Dr. Smiles and again I waited to hear from him. I called back and gave the receptionist the telephone number and the fax number of the prescription plan so that a new prescription could be sent to me. Now that I understood that I was to take the decreased amount I no longer felt pressured to get the supplemental amount to add up to the three-month allotment.

CHAPTER 23 – *Nadiva*

My granddaughter Nadiva celebrated her first birthday on May 21st 2005. Mollie, Carl, Nadiva, Michael, Eddie and I visited the children's garden of NYU Hospital. I was taken there in the wheelchair. The plants were beautifully kept. They had paintings on the wall. It was a little playground setting with tricycles, a swing, small tables and chairs for the children and some big ones for the adults, and a caged rabbit. There were ramps with different levels for the children to play on. Nadiva was delighted to explore. She had just started to walk. We were all delighted to have her first birthday celebration together at the hospital in such a very happy setting. We had birthday cake and gifts for Nadiva. I would have liked to run around and play with her, but at this point I knew it was not possible in my current physical state and I was happy to be blessed to sit down and watch the happiness of my family together.

Nadiva is now over a year and a half. How she has grown! She has a small vocabulary. She understands everything that is spoken to her. She walks beautifully. She dances, sings, plays, and practices making faces in the mirror. I have grown much stronger and my balance is quite good, considering that my right leg does not respond normally to stimuli. The feeling of balance in my right side is not the way I would want it to be yet. I was able to baby-sit for Nadiva. She's such a happy child. It was a delight for me. I was able to "run" around with her, and sing and dance together, and sit down together on the floor and explore together the world of toys and books. Happiness brings spiritual and physical health. It is my wish that all of us in the future will have more happiness and good health.

CHAPTER 24 - Terrace flower pot garden

I love plants, have always kept plants in my home and outside my home. They are a part of life. I like to take care of my garden myself. There's a special feeling when I participate in this activity. On my second floor terrace I have a flower pot garden. Every winter I bring the houseplants inside. You can see from the outside the geraniums peeping through the sunny attic windows. While I was still in the hospital the weather started to get warm enough to bring them outside. Michael had been taking care of watering the plants while I was in the hospital.

In June Michael carried out the plants back to the terrace. Every year when the plants would be placed outside on the porch they welcomed the sun. Michael continued to care for them even when I returned home, until I was able to care for them myself a few weeks later. The plants had grown so well during their time in the winter, they needed to be repotted. That was a big job and I needed some help. The plants were heavy and they needed to be separated and mixtures of loam and fertilizer and potting soil had to be added. I had to find a new place for their new larger containers. Some were lined atop the brick fence, some were on the floor, and others were seated on top of plant stands. I enjoyed designing the space. When I was in Rusk in the occupational therapy department, plant therapy was used as part of the healing program. I have always used that as part of my personal healing program. It gives me pleasure to be part of the process of bringing life and beauty to the environment. Taking care of the plants, weeding and watering, makes an additional bonus to move my hands and make them more flexible and strong. The plants continued to prosper all fall until Thanksgiving approached, when the weather turned cold again. I was able to make cuttings to share with my neighbors and daughter, who appreciated their beauty. It was time to bring them back into the house.

CHAPTER 25 – Violin

When I was three I was introduced to the violin. A neighbor was an orchestra conductor. I would listen and fall asleep listening to him play the violin in the evening. One day when I was four he asked if I would like to play the violin. Of course I said yes. He brought out a tiny quarter sized violin. He laid a deep red velvet cloth on the piano bench and placed the violin upon it. Thus began my love affair with the violin.

So began the ritual of washing the hands. The hands had to be completely scrubbed and cleaned. My teacher, Mr. Gordon, inspected them and gave his approval before starting the lesson. My first lesson was holding the violin. With great care I lifted the precious instrument and placed it under my chin and then put it down on the velvet cloth. When my teacher was satisfied that I was able to hold it with comfort and great respect, I was able to continue. The lessons were a source of love. My teacher and I loved each other. Through the violin we were able to share a common love. In subsequent lessons he taught me how to hold the bow. He tuned my ear. He focused on my ability to concentrate and to listen to the sound. He had done exercises with me to improve these abilities to perfect pitch. He taught me to read music. Fractions became part of my language. He insisted that I learn the piano as well as the violin. I still remember the book of *Hammond Piano Exercises*. As a reward for doing well in my lessons, Mr. Gordon made the best chocolate egg cream (e'crème) soda for me. My teacher saw me as his protégée. When he was not on tour I would spend hours practicing with him. I was not so interested to practice on my own. He made it a delight to study. When he passed away near my sixth birthday part of my world fell apart. I never had a teacher like him to instill such a love of learning. I continued studying the violin through my school years. On and off through my life I would continue to play; sometimes many years would go without practicing. A year and a half ago I accidentally broke my wrist and I had a yearning to use my violin as part of my therapy. I tried to hold the violin in the proper position. It was a struggle. My arm, wrist and fingers were not working together. I put it aside for a time when I felt I would have more patience and dexterity. In the meantime, I became ill with vasculitis and a subsequent stroke. While attending occupational therapy I had in mind that I would want again to work with the violin. At home I took out my violin from the closet and lovingly opened the worn case, but inside the red velvet was the object of my love. The mellow wood with its beautiful grain drew me to it. It felt good to hold it in my hand. I tried to make my fingers work again. Holding the violin is very involved. It must have the alignment of the hands, wrist, elbow and shoulders. The fine motor skills have to be working with great dexterity for the fingers to be able to stretch and reach and make the correct placement of the fingers while wrapping around the neck of the violin. I blew into my tuning pipe and checked each string. Each string has to be individually tuned by turning a dowel that holds it in place on the neck of the violin. There are two dowels on each side. In order to manipulate them you have to make fine movements in a small space. Sometimes the tension of the string unwinds and you have to start all over again. I picked up the violin in my left hand and placed it under my chin. My hands were caressing the strings. My right hand index finger was placed on the keyboard, ready to pluck. We start with the sound of the "A" string and continue on to the E, D, and G-strings. They are called open strings and do not require the pressure of the fingers to play their note. I tried to play the notes that required pressure. It was hard work. At first it was difficult to reach the D and G strings. I practiced for ten minutes. The veins in my wrist bulged with the effort but I felt satisfaction that I was able to do that much. I realized that my success would be measured in minute increments.

The violin has to be held in the correct posture, aligning the fingers, wrist, elbow, shoulder, and neck. I opened the music book I had borrowed from the library and thought I would try to play, but all I saw were dots; I could not make heads or tails of the symbols. From my experience I know that the notes are written on a staff and I remember the mnemonic "every good boy does fine" for the lines and "face" for the spaces. I was unable to connect the seeing of the notes with the comprehension. It felt like too much information at once. I called up my sister Phillis to help guide me. She was very helpful and sent me an email with a link to beginning music that had the staff and sounds. I pondered this for a while and was able to rebuild some connections in my brain. I continued to practice reading the music, attempting to find the correct fingering while trying to pluck the notes with the index finger of the right hand. It takes a lot of coordination and thought because the neck of the violin, where you place the fingers of your left hand, has no markings or delineations as with the fret of the guitar. Because the feeling in my right hand was not working, I had to consciously and constantly see where I had to place my hands, while at the same time reading the music. I felt so accomplished when I could repeat a phrase that I had to call Phillis and show off. She was delighted to hear my progress. I continue to progress in very small increments. I can actually see where in the future it will sound like recognizable music.

CHAPTER 26 – *Computer*

For my birthday I got a wonderful gift, a computer, from my sister Esther. When I had been working, the computer was part of my tools. I had familiarity and a basic knowledge of the tasks I needed for work. Michael opened the box for me and set up the computer, keyboard, and monitor on my desk. I should have been ready to start. I could not make heads or tails of how to operate it. At this point my head would not compute. Michael had to take me step by step, how to turn on the computer, and how to use the mouse. I waited for the desktop's opening screen. Michael arranged the screen so it would be organized to show the functions I would use most. He showed me how to access my documents and how to get on the Internet to retrieve my email. This took a series of lessons because it was as if it was brand new and I had to practice in order to utilize the commands. I had to learn how to use the mouse. There are three buttons on the mouse. The one on the left is the main button. It allows you to choose an action; the center is a scroll bar, and the right chooses various options according to the program it is working.

Commands can be given via the mouse or by typing a series of keys. My right hand maneuvered the mouse. I had to hold the three points of contact individually when I wanted to choose the different functions. I had to hold the mouse and control my finger to press each button individually to follow my commands. I had to strain my brain to remember how to access the commands by using the keys. For example: the command "**ctrl c**" for copy. My hands used to know the keyboard. I used to touch type. Now I have to memorize the keyboard. Now I have to look at every letter before typing it. When I tried to depress the key on the right side, my fingers had a mind of their own. They seem to want to go to a different place, my middle and ring fingers in particular. All of a sudden when I depress the letter **l** the ring finger moves by itself to stay on the letter **m**. When I look at the keys I see the correct placement of my fingers on the keys. It is as if my fingers are playing hide and seek as soon as my eyes turn away. This is very frustrating, especially when I want to go on the computer and use my password to access the internet. I can't see the letters I am typing. They are hidden by the asterisks so I don't know if I'm typing correctly. I think I am and after seven or eight times, I actually am allowed to enter the internet. This is a necessary daily ritual.

Bright and early at six A.M., Sunday to Friday, my sister Phillis telephoned me to help start writing about the process of my illness and recovery. The night before and/or that morning, I would jot a list of topics to write about. Phillis listened as I dictated. She wrote on her computer as I flushed out my jottings. My sister Phillis lives in Saratoga Springs, NY. The computer made our long distance correspondence possible. Her help was invaluable. At first she complained that her typing was slow. My comeback was that my speech was slow too, so it was an even match. We laughed as we struggled together. It was fun. Each day there was a sense of accomplishment.

Phillis emailed the work we completed each day. I read it and downloaded it to my documents. Sometimes I find special problems in accessing the commands on the screen. It appeared to me that I was unable to find the download button. After playing around on the computer screen for several hours I discovered that the previous screen could be enlarged by pulling down the handles to hold and enlarge the top screen. There it was; the download button magically appeared. It was hidden, and by increasing the size it showed the full page. Phillis told me that another way to increase the page size is to press the button on the top right of the screen next to the 'X'.

Thank goodness Phillis is sitting at the keyboard. I could never do it without her help.

I have expressive (the ability to say), and affective (the ability to comprehend) types of aphasia. I also have a neural disconnect between my vision and hearing. As a consequence, I can't spell. I hear a word one way and visualize it in another way. Often I type syllables in an incorrect order and am not aware of my mistake because in my head I think I have sounded it out correctly. In the same way, I confuse individual letters. Spell check is a wonderful device but it does not go far enough for my needs, because I can't spell enough of the words to make it work. However, it does give me clues. If I try enough combinations I may hit the right one. I have been relying a lot on a dictionary. It has lots of words to choose from. Sometimes I get lucky.

The American Stroke Association tells us about that:

Wernicke's Aphasia (receptive)

People with serious comprehension difficulties have what is called Wernicke's aphasia and:

- Often say many words that don't make sense.

- May fail to realize they are saying the wrong words; for instance, they might call a fork a "gleeble."

- May string together a series of meaningless words that sound like a sentence but don't make sense.

- Have challenges because our dictionary of words is shelved in a similar region of the left hemisphere, near the area used for understanding words.

Broca's Aphasia (expressive)

When a stroke injures the frontal regions of the left hemisphere, different kinds of language problems can occur. This part of the brain is important for putting words together to form complete sentences. Injury to the left frontal area can lead to what is called Broca's aphasia. Survivors with Broca's aphasia:

- Can have great difficulty forming complete sentences.
- May get out some basic words to get their message across, but leave out words like "is" or "the."
- Often say something that doesn't resemble a sentence.
- Can have trouble understanding sentences.
- Can make mistakes in following directions like left, right, under, and after.

Car bump boom! This is not a complete sentence, but it certainly expresses an important idea. Sometimes these individuals will say a word that is close to what they intend, but not the exact word; for example they may say "car" when they mean "truck."

A speech pathologist friend mentioned to a patient that she was having a bad day. She said, "I was bitten by a dog." The stroke survivor asked, "Why did you do that?" In this conversation, the patient understood the basic words spoken, but failed to realize that the words of the sentence and the order of the words were critical to interpreting the correct meaning of the sentence, that the dog bit the woman and not vice versa.

Remember, when someone has aphasia:

- It is important to make the distinction between language and intelligence.

- Many people mistakenly think they are not as smart as they used to be.

- Their problem is that they cannot use language to communicate what they know.

- They can think; they just can't *say* what they think.

CHAPTER 27 - *More speech therapy*

I thought I could continue to bring my speech back to pre-stroke level by speaking with others, by careful listening, reading aloud, and watching and listening to television with text. After six months of struggling, I started looking for a teacher.

I've been working with an excellent speech therapist, Susan Weg. She recognized my inability to form clearly enunciated and articulated speech as one of my prime problems. She gave me homework assignments to help overcome the impediment. She asked me to read aloud stories and newspaper articles, to listen to the new words. And to write as if I were writing a diary with attention to the content and spelling of each word. She asked me to use three to five sentences daily. Now, that sounds like it should be a cinch; after all what is three to five sentences? But no, I have news for you: finding the right words and right spelling and the actual tasks of writing and decent penmanship so that it could be read back is very involved. I hope with her help and with the exercises we work on I will in the future be able to master this. We worked on **breathing properly**.

Exercise to demonstrate level of breathing:
Shallow breathing
Place hands on chest. Breathe only to the level of your hands. It feels like panting.
Middle (Thoracic) breathing
Place hands on the base of the rib cage. Breathe only to the level of your hands.
Breathing thoracic is less taxing than shallow breathing.
Deep full breathing
Place hands just below the navel. Breathe only to the level of your hands.
The diaphragm is able to extend to its limit.
Deep abdominal breathing is the most efficient and least taxing of the three. As a deep breathing bonus, the diaphragm massages the organs in the abdominal cavity (intestines…)

Speech is produced during exhalation using full diaphragmatic breaths. When I become unsure of myself or emotional I falter and appear to be stuttering. She calmly and slowly models the taking of a breath and I repeat, usually with much more satisfactory results. There are times when it is not possible to make the desired result, where my brain is not able to make a certain connection. At this time I have to use other strategies and search for words with similar meanings. One strategy is trying to find the letter and sound that's giving me difficulty by saying the alphabet in my head so that I can listen to the sounds and try to produce them. This technique also works in trying to spell the words.

Breathing is something we take for granted from the first breath as a newborn. Babies take full breaths all the way through the belly. As we get older we don't always breathe efficiently. We usually hear "breathe through the diaphragm". Today most people breathe in a very shallow way. You can feel that when you are panting. The neck locks up and makes the words come out with difficulty. The neck and upper body become stressed. Alexander, an orator, lost his voice. Through his suffering from incorrect breathing and posture, he was able to restore his voice and founded the Alexander Technique. We are so used to incorrect breathing that we take it as normal. Thoracic breathing takes less energy as you breathe through the middle area of the back and still less as you take fuller and fuller breaths from the abdomen. You can hear it in the timber of your voice. I used to be able to sing with great strength; now I have the problem of breathing shallowly. I was unaware of this. I needed to have this pointed out to me by my speech therapist. I've been having difficulty following her direction to simply breathe in and out, to know the difference what is in and out. We do some exercises to help me be aware of this. Maybe I am stubborn or maybe I am having real difficulty realizing the sequences and feelings of breathing properly.

This may have something to do with my apraxia. In any case I have to overcome this. I need further instruction to enable me to process the breathing route.

Hearing me speak with my impediment, which people perceive as a handicap, leads people to believe that my brain function and mind are impaired. To a degree they are right. My vasculitis and stroke left me with considerable damage, which is healing as evidenced by the fact that my speech and balance are returning. The National Aphasia Association Bookmark says "aphasia is a loss of words, not intelligence. My mind works perfectly well; I just have difficulty communicating." At Rusk, where the staff was used to dealing with this type of injury, they were patient and understanding. When I came out of the hospital and people heard my speech, they wanted to help. They did not understand what I needed help with. They did not understand that what I needed was for them to understand that I understood their speech perfectly well. They continually wanted to slow down their speech to match mine. They would speak to me as if I had a loss of hearing and a loss of comprehension. One day, after synagogue, I was standing with a group of ladies when one spoke to me using speech that mimicked mine. I became angry and let her know that I was not addlepated, that I did not have a problem with understanding her speech, but I did have a problem that she did not understand. The problem was communicating, not thinking. A friend came to visit me; she had another reaction. She knew that I could communicate with my speech. She wanted to help me walk. I found that amusing since I could walk much better than she. She wanted to hold my arm and especially wanted to help me down the stairs. When dealing with people in a business situation on the telephone, some people become very impatient. I found that the way to deal with this is to tell them that I have a handicap and that I appreciate their patience.

CHAPTER 28 - Transportation

Shoes are made for walking. When discussing my means of transportation with the speech therapist I told her that I walk wherever I have to go locally. It's .7 of a mile to my therapist's home. My legs are looking good. I live about half a mile from the Long Island Railroad Station. My shoes take me there also. Getting the ticket and taking the train to get to Esther's to make the doctor's appointment involves many steps. There are many choices to make when buying your ticket from the newly installed ticket machines. The first time I tried to use it I was so frustrated that I asked a fellow passenger to do it for me. As I became braver I tried it on my own. You had to know which station to leave from and which one to arrive at, how many tickets do you use, peak or non-peak, disabled or senior citizen credit or cash, do you want a receipt, and then you reach into the slot and take out your freshly printed ticket. There are no longer human beings to greet you and wish you a good journey. I boarded the Long Island Railroad train and met my sister at the *Flatbush Avenue* stop. From there we drove to Manhattan's NYU Medical Center for various tests, most recently an MRI and MRA. Esther drove around the block to find a parking lot. It's amazing how expensive it is to park. It cost 18 dollars for 2 hours. On the way into the hospital I mentioned that it would be very nice to visit with my occupational therapist. We walked through the long lobby to the hallway with the elevator to the radiology unit where I was seen for the MRI (magnetic resonance imaging) and MRA (magnetic resonance of arteries). The tests ran back to back and did not take long, about half an hour in total. Filling out the paperwork and waiting time took much longer than the tests themselves. On the way back, while walking through the corridors, Esther said wouldn't it be nice if we were able see the occupational therapist on the way out because we were limited on time. Her office was on the third floor and she just happened to be on the first floor on the way to a meeting. As fate would have it we bumped into her. She gave me her email address and said she thought she still had my phone number. I looked forward to our contact. Esther took me back to the railroad. I had enough time to comfortably get my return ticket and relax on the train during my trip back. The only exercise that I had this day was the walk to and from the train station. I thought that I should have more energy but I felt drained by the day's activities. It was enough to think of it and prepare dinner before going to sleep.

CHAPTER 29 - Feeling the stress

There was a lot of tension back at work. All the faculty of the school was feeling it. It was to be reorganized into different schools, which meant that everyone working in the present school was going to be excessed and would have to be relocated. It put a tremendous strain not only on the teachers but on the students as well. It was difficult to teach and difficult to learn in this atmosphere. Everybody had his or her private stress and strain as well. My house was in the process of renovation and I had to deal with workmen. I was the contractor for the job. It started out to be a very simple project but it became a big can of worms. It took over a good part of my life. Part of it was fun; the rest was very taxing to say the least. But I learned a lot about construction and I learned how to handle and work with the workmen. As I look back it was a lot to carry on my shoulders. I wish in retrospect that I was more capable and had some more support.

Until we go through the same kind of experience we don't know how other people feel. I'm currently receiving social security disability from the government and disability from my work; together it would cover my necessary expenses and nothing else. However, because I am on disability from work, they give me only a partial payment each month until I get a letter from work stating the award. This takes up to six months. For that time I have to borrow on my mortgage in order to survive. To me this is a wonderful way for the board of education to make interest on money. When the appropriate amount of money will be awarded it's supposed to take care of the arrears. I never truly understood the financial struggles of other people who have disabilities or illnesses or other types of problems until now. I understood it intellectually but never felt it. I cannot go on occasion to a restaurant for a meal. I cannot occasionally go to the theatre. I cannot stop in to buy new clothing. I cannot partake in community events that you have to pay for, no matter how small the amount is. When I want to give a birthday gift to a family member or close friend I cannot. I used to give donations to charities continually and I cannot do that either. It's a good thing that I don't have such an expensive life style, but there is a point where you try to live on a subsistence allowance. You think that you are doing okay until the bills actually catch up to you. I am happy at this point that I am still able to have my home. I am looking forward to the warmer weather when I can get some relief from the heating bills. I walk around my home with at least two sweaters. I keep the heat no more than sixty-five degrees and only in the part of my house that I am using. One of my bathrooms I usually keep at sixty degrees. I'm trying to conserve. The heating bills have almost doubled in this last year. It looks to me as though the economy has stabilized by an increase in fuel costs. It doesn't matter how much of a raise you get because it will cost more in the store. I feel as though I am not allowed the good things in life.

CHAPTER 30 - My feelings this morning

motivation

organization

time

energy

sum up my feelings this morning

I usually am very motivated. I want very positive outcomes in my daily life. I am trying to take on more responsibility and in general learn more, and still allow myself time to socialize. I don't think I have enough time to do all this efficiently. I know that I have to focus on what is most important but all these things feel like they are most important, so how do I choose? For years I have been saying, "If only I didn't have to sleep." But sleep is important and, until I learn the secret of performing without sleep, I have to consider sleep an important part of my life. Sometimes I just want to do nothing, but then what is it I do when I say I want to do nothing? There is always something to do. I'm very pleased that I want to take more responsibility and am able to focus on that. Physically I am holding the pen with my right hand, which is quite an accomplishment. I'm able to fill out the information on the check and sign my name. I'm still having trouble spelling, particularly spelling out numbers. My speech therapist noted my problem with spelling, numbers and gave me homework where I practiced writing numbers one through twenty. That gave me the motivation to try writing checks. I still have to learn how to write one hundred. I was too lazy to look up the word hundred in the dictionary. I did not care. I thought to myself the people receiving the check would be able to laugh and deposit it even with my poor spelling. Another new thing

I tried was to sew a button on my coat. The button on the top of my collar had been missing for almost all this past season. I used a scarf to hold my collar closed. I took out my sewing box. From it I took a spool of heavy thread and a needle. I had an assortment of needles. Most of them were too small for the thread. As I kept looking I decided I needed a thinner thread. Finally I matched up a wide needle with the thread. I cut the thread on a slant to make it easier for me to pull the thread through the eye of the needle. I was very pleased with my hand-eye coordination. I had not known that I would be able to see that well again. I measured the thread to twice the length of my arm and made a knot. I had not done this in over a year. I had the occasion to help some students learn how to sew during my counseling sessions and was surprised to find that these middle school students did not know how to knot thread. I first had to stay stitch the material around the place for the button and then I sewed on the button. I looked at my accomplishment and smiled. Of course these two things took an enormous amount of time and effort. Each one takes about half a day to accomplish. I do understand that I have to be patient with myself, but the understanding and the doing are not always in sync. I feel guilty when I don't accomplish what I feel is enough; for example, when I don't finish reading a book, and I have to renew it at the library. When I plan to practice my violin more and do more dance and yoga exercises, when I don't bake the cookies even though I prepare the ingredients to make them, when my house is not dusted and cleaned the way I would like it to be as often as I would like it to be, and when I think of the garden and how I will manage everything. I'm happy I can manage to clean up the waste that ends up on the lawn of my corner house. It takes at least an hour to clear that away.

Motivation comes in funny ways; because I talked about making Hamantashen cookies, I decided to make them. My family planned to visit me and I pulled out the rolling pin and all the ingredients and pulled out the cookbook, and had a good time putting the ingredients together. I shaped the dough into three-cornered hats, and filled them with prune filling. I glazed them with egg and popped them into the oven. They smelled so good I knew they were ready. Everybody enjoyed the treat the next day when they visited.

It was so great to see Michael, Mollie, Nadiva, Esther, and Aiden (Esther's four- year-old grandson) again. We had lunch and went outside to the playground. When we came back to my home we played with the children and their toys. They explored every inch of my apartment. They climbed the spiral stairs to the attic and they felt very cozy with the big open space and the slanted walls of the attic bringing the height down to them. Michael put together the shopping cart that Esther brought for Nadiva. They carried the shopping cart and plastic food and cash register, microwave and tea set upstairs and had a blast. It was delightful to see the two children playing together. It was delightful to see my family all together. The joy I had lasted through the next day with the excitement of the eustress, but when they are not with me there is a loneliness. A cloud comes over my emotions, even though it cheers me to speak to my family on the telephone; it is not the same as having them with me. I'm very happy for them and I have great pride in them. My children are adults and they have to make their own way, and I have to carry on in my way. In years past when my children and I lived together it seemed it would never end and as if I would always have someone in the house with me. **How I looked forward to creating a balance with some alone space**. My loneliness fades as I continue to do the many activities of daily living.

People have told me that I have courage. I did not see that. The dictionary tells me that courage is meeting danger even when you do fear; bravery; acting as one believes one should. I didn't see anything brave or courageous in being sick. I just wanted to get better.

When I see people in the news who put their lives on the line for others, I look at them as being brave and courageous; but actually, when people are interviewed they also don't see that they are doing something out of the ordinary. They just had to do what they felt was necessary. **The act of living is courageous.**

CHAPTER 31 - Spirituality

Although my time seems to be less flexible, it is filled. One time I went with Mollie to a learning symposium where I was asked what I want to get out of this experience. It seemed to me that the focus was on becoming more responsible for yourself, not blaming others for yourself, and basically growing up while being a viable part of the human community. We broke into smaller groups. The guide asked us what we wanted to learn from this program. I told her that I wanted to be more spiritual. I always felt a need for spirituality. She said this is not the place for me. She said the focus of this symposium was learning to be responsible. I am a responsible person.

I've always been a spiritual person and since my illness I have had time to find resources within my community. On any given day there are lectures dealing with the understanding of our place in the world through the works of the Jewish religion. Through the Five Books of Moses, the Psalms, the Prophets, the Oral Law, and the commentaries, no matter how many times you hear the lecturers they always have something new to relate to the community and the individual. There's always another aspect to delve into, another way to look at the same old thing. It's a plan for the big picture of life and it's our job to uncover it.

We each have our own God-given gifts. When I was on the operating table at NYU, having the angiogram and the massive stroke, God gave me the gift of life again. I felt that there must be a purpose for this second chance. Although I focus on getting well, I'm trying to understand what the real purpose is. What did I have to do that was still undone, or is there something I never thought of that my experience will lead to? I have an appreciation of what God has given me; my family, my community, the splendor of nature, and my talents and gifts. How do I put them together and be worthy of this gift? I keep feeling that I should be making a difference. Maybe I'm looking at it the wrong way; I don't know. I know that more often than not, the differences are not great; they come in small increments and while you are in the process it's hard to see, like when you see a child growing every day you don't see the changes. So here I am trying to work on my speech, my physical therapy, relate to my family and community, appreciate and relate to nature, while trying to write the story of my experience. Oh God what am I supposed to do? Give me some understanding so that at least I know I am on the right track. My sister Phillis tells me that she's not doing anything today, that when she finishes helping me write she will prepare the challahs for today, she will sort her mail which has been waiting for days, she will see to her grandson and daughter-in-law's needs since they are both feeling ill, and she will go to the synagogue where she will help prepare challahs for a hunger drive. Yesterday she visited a sick neighbor and took pictures of him and will send them to his wife in Israel. She will go food shopping with her husband, spend some time with her grandson, and prepare for the Sabbath. Thank God the daylight is growing longer so that she will have time to prepare. She really feels that she is not doing anything. It is so much a part of what she does every day that she does not consider it. So what do people really do when they say that they're doing 'nothing'? When I help people by counseling them or showing them some exercises, or I do the laundry, or shop, or clean my house; what are those things? Are they important in God's eyes? Dear God, please give me understanding so that I will be pleasing to you.

    Passover is approaching. It will be the anniversary of the day I became ill and was taken to the hospital. It makes me wonder if I had used my time well. I wonder what the future holds in store. My very good friend in whose home I celebrated the holy day last year invited me again. I invited my children to be with me at my home. I thanked her but declined as I told her I was afraid of a repeat performance. She said lightning doesn't strike in the same place twice. I don't want lightning to strike anyplace.

PART TWO

CHAPTER 1 - *Opportunities for Jewish learning; learning with Esther*

5-12-08

The Rockaway peninsula has a varied population. In the 11691 zip code area, the 2010 census population showed a total 60,025 people comprised of: Black, White, Hispanic or Latino, Asian, Asian Indian, American Indian, and Alaskan Native peoples. The eastern section of Far Rockaway, bordering on Nassau County, has a large Jewish population (mainly White).

The part of Far Rockaway I live in has changed over the last thirty years. It always had an orthodox Jewish community, but there are degrees of orthodoxy. The religious schools, yeshivas, were at one time a choice of coed or non-coed schools. They have all become either male or female schools because there is a philosophy that learning is better when the focus is not distracted by gender.

Before I became ill, I would enjoy celebrating the Sabbath by going to services, having the festive meal with friends, and going to a *shiur*, a lecture, on a topic generally relating to the *parsha* or portion of the Torah that was read during the religious service. In this community you could have several choices of *shiurim*/lectures. Each lecturer tried to bring out different points. At the Congregation Kneseth Israel, they rotate women lecturers for a female audience. It's amazing to me how many different aspects there are to learn about in each parsha (chapter) and how the lecturer can make these aspects come to life and make it meaningful for today. One person who was lecturing was particularly instructive. I heard her speak before I got sick. After the shiur I asked her to clarify points. She saw my enthusiasm and offered to me the opportunity to learn with her. I thought I would like to learn with her but I also thought she had some growing to do before we could actually connect. Now during my recovery I heard her speak again and felt this is the time. She said she was very busy and suggested that I go learn with someone else, and she would suggest other people. I said no, she is the one; and with that she accepted and made time for me. And so Esther Wein became my *chavrusa*, my teacher and learning partner. For a year thereafter we learned together.

5-13-08

Wednesday morning I would get up, say my prayers, have breakfast, walk about a little more than half a mile from my house to Esther Wein's house, and get there at approximately a quarter of nine. By that time Esther had her five children off to school and she was able to start teaching me. It was very gracious of her to take the time because, not only does she have a full teaching schedule, but she was also in the middle of house renovations. With the constant flow of workmen in and out, it was an exciting atmosphere. Esther asked me what I would like to learn, so I told her I wanted to learn the meaning of the prayers in the prayer book. I felt that was a good place to begin. One question led to another and before you knew it we were integrating topics in the Torah because the prayer books are related to all the teachings of the Torah. I learned how important the Oral Torah is and I appreciated having such a learned person guiding me. Sometimes we started out studying in her very comfortable library. Sometimes I went with her on errands and we learned along the way. Sometimes we took breaks to do some yoga and Pilate exercises. I was honored to also be included in learning with her father-in-law, Zalmon Wein who was a Torah scholar. I was included with the family on many Shabbos luncheons, where there were lively discussions in a very down to earth atmosphere. Esther's time was getting more and more filled with many commitments. She started me off on a very good path to continue my learning. I no longer studied with her but did attend her weekly lectures. During this time, I was doing a lot of walking. I walked to Esther's house, and I walked to my speech therapists, which was also a considerable distance. I was very happy to be physically able to do this walking. However, as I continued with my walking, I found it getting more and more difficult and extremely painful. I kept walking because I wanted to go places independently. I didn't want to admit the extent of my pain to myself, and certainly not to others.

CHAPTER 2 - *The library*

After my hospitalization, though I still have my driver's license, I gave up driving. I no longer felt safe on the road and gave my car away. I continued traveling by foot. I was stubborn and I was able to disregard my body's communication to me until there was no way I could go on without help. I had reached a point of such severe pain that it was difficult to take steps within my own home. One of my walking destinations was the library. I was a regular. I enjoyed the video collection. I viewed them as my dinner theater. By using the subtitle feature, I was also able to work on my reading skills, combining the multidiscipline modes of sight and sound. The library was also a wonderful source of knowledge for me, especially for books pertaining to healing the body. I particularly focused on the spine, neck, head, and nerves that innervate the muscles. I have a holistic outlook. I engage my spiritual and physical being. The reference librarian was very helpful. I was able to borrow technical books from libraries across the state.

CHAPTER 3 - Walking with pain

The weather had become warmer; it was the beginning of March. I was so happy to take off some of my layers of clothing. I peeled off my hat, my gloves, my scarf, my jacket, my boots and my stockings. Now I am wearing my sweater and vest, socks, and sneakers.

I've been finding that my back is painful. Little by little, the walk to the library became more and more difficult. It took longer and longer to get there. I had to stop several times on each block to sit on a stoop or lean against a pole or fence. The day came when I could not make it past my house.

The last visit I had with Dr. Smiles I told him I was having pain in my lower back and it was radiating to other parts of my back and leg. I emailed my doctor, asking him for help, telling him I was in such excruciating pain. Help, help! I made an appointment. My sister took me to the doctor.

I told him where the pain originated. I was having pain in my lower back and it was radiating to other parts of my back and leg.

He immediately sent me for an x-ray of my back and pelvic area. There was a radiology laboratory conveniently located in the same building as Dr. Smile's office. Esther and I waited an hour for my turn. It took no time once I was in. I wanted to see the x-ray picture. The technician was kind enough to show it to me and pointed out the area of the spine that looked misaligned.

I saw exactly what I had described to the doctor that I felt in my pain. It showed impingement of the nerve of the fourth and fifth lumbar vertebrae, which were very much out of alignment. I realized that this was due to my inability to receive neural sensation on my right side. Thank God there was nothing wrong showing in the pelvic area. My posture appeared to be excellent to everyone who saw me; for a while, me too. So much for appearances!

I couldn't understand why the radiologist was taking so long to send the report to my doctor, since it was only a short distance from one office to another. It took over a week for it to arrive. Dr. Smiles prescribed physical therapy for me and sent me the prescription and a copy of the report to show to the physical therapist. I went to the physical therapy twice a week for several months. The first session was to evaluate and tell me how the therapy would proceed. First they would give me heat and electrical stimulation; then the therapist would give me ten minutes of massage and then follow up with an exercise trainer who would give me specific exercises to help my condition. The trainer watched to make sure I did it correctly, and then moved on to other people--unless I called him to instruct me about the next part. The therapist gave me pictures with exercises so I could continue working on these exercises at home.

I realized that I was getting worse, not better.

The next time I saw the physical therapist he asked how I was doing. I told him that I had a problem with pain when I was walking home from my therapy. It was so bad that I had to stop and find a step to sit on until the pain passed. The pain goes through my back all the way through my toes. We changed the game plan and tried stimulation and massage for the last part of the session. When I was finished with the physical therapy I took some time to rest before I walked home.

It's a good thing it was warm weather! I could comfortably wear only backless open-toed shower shoes. My left foot was in pain. It was very difficult for me to keep the right shoe on without feeling my right side. I didn't know if the shoe was still on my foot. I would realize that the shoe was lost when I would glance at my bare foot and then go back several steps to find my misplaced shoe.

Halfway through my walk I had to stop completely. I tried to stretch my back in different positions. A car pulled into a driveway directly in front of me and the driver asked if I was ok. I did not want to complain and when he asked me a couple of times more I thought better and told him I needed some help. He asked me if he could drive me home. I gratefully accepted. I needed to rest.

Exercise to stretch the spine:
1. Stand or sit in alignment with feet spaced shoulder width under the hips, hands at your sides hanging freely from the shoulders. Engage the abdomen (feel like the navel touches the back). Slowly lower the head, neck, shoulders, one vertebra at a time lowering chin to chest. Take a deep breath. Hold the stretch. Exhale. Feel the upper spine. Slowly (in order to avoid dizziness) unroll the spine; lifting the shoulders, then neck, and head back into place. Breathe.
2. Repeat 1; Place hands on thighs near your knees, slowly lower back until hands reach the knees. Raise the spine one vertebra at a time till hands are mid-thigh level.
3. Repeat 1; slowly lower and raise the spine one vertebra at a time to the lower back. Hands go to the level of the calves.
4. Repeat 1; while standing with knees straight, slowly lower the spine as far as you are able, dangling the arms, stretching the **hamstrings.** Unroll slowly back to standing position.
5. Or continue hamstring stretch, placing hands on calves or ankles if you are able. Breathe. Place both hands on the left calf or ankle and twist your torso close to your left leg. Breathe. Place hands on ankles or calves. Breathe.

Repeat to the right.
Stand up slowly--Bend the knees slightly. Do not allow the knees to extend beyond the toes.
Slowly straighten knees and rest of the body.

> **Exercise – Spinal twist 1:**
> 1. Stand or sit in alignment with feet spaced under the hips.
> 2. Standing--Bend the knees slightly.
> 3. Reach your right hand across to your left hip.
> 4. Reach your left hand behind your back to your right hip.
> 5. Turn your head as far as you can to the left while keeping your upper body vertical. Feel like a cork screw.
> 6. Take a deep breath.
> 7. Release the arms and head. Untwist the spine. If standing, straighten the knees.
> 8. Breathe;
> Repeat exercise twisting to the right.
>
> **Spinal twist 2:**
> Spinal twist for lower back (Helpful for sciatica)
> Sit centered on a straight back chair.
> Sit tall on your ischium (sit bones) and use your abdominal muscles. Breathe.
> 1. Cross legs from the hip. Right place foot on top. Turn torso left like corkscrew toward the back of the chair. Breathe.
> 2. Return to center.
> 3. Repeat 1 and 2, turning right.
>
> Repeat exercise (1, 2, and 3) crossing the legs from the hip with the left foot on top. Note: Also, walking tall (using abdominal muscles) takes strain off the pelvic girdle.

5-14-08

I decided something different had to be done. I started looking for an alternative. I was researching where to find a Doctor of Osteopathy. I found one locally and made an appointment. A DO doctor is a medical doctor who specializes in correcting alignment with a combination of physical therapy and chiropractic. Dr. Joyce intently listened to my history and proceeded to examine me. He saw how very tender my body was and said he would not touch me any further without seeing an MRI. He gave me the prescription for the MRI and some very strong medication to relax the muscles in order to relieve some of the pain. I made the appointment immediately for the MRI. I went back to Dr. Joyce with the results. It was very clear to the doctor that there was so much pressure on my spine due to the misalignment of the spine and impinged nerves that he could see the severity of my pain. In no uncertain terms he recommended that I not go to a chiropractor and stop physical therapy immediately. He strongly recommended that I see a surgeon. He gave me two recommendations of surgeons. I told him I am not going for surgery. He said, "Then at least see what they have to say." I was very resistant. I went to Dr. Smiles with a copy of the MRI. Dr. Smiles agreed with Dr. Joyce that surgery was absolutely necessary. I said, "No." Dr. Smiles said then, "at least you can have a spinal injection, some sort of cortisone, to block the pain."

"It seems to me that the reason for this problem had been my inability to feel sensation, and now that I am getting some sensations back, even though they are of pain, you want me to take them away. I'd rather feel the pain and deal with it." And I did.

CHAPTER 4 - Alternative techniques

The pain continued to be great. I realized that pain medication is something I do not want to become addicted to, so I cut that out very quickly. Dr. Smiles said that a couple of Advil would be alright. I have been training all of my life for dance. I am very aware of my body. It was time for me to depend on my own inner strength and knowledge. I worked out by just trying different ways of moving my body, taking note of the effect of each part on the other. I looked into acupuncture. I had been studying various methods of pain relief: acupressure, a form of shiatsu, yoga, Pilates, and dance.

5-15-08

Acupuncture is a system of inserting needles into energy points. I was always afraid of this procedure. I don't like any needles stuck into me. But, when you get to a point of that much pain, you are willing to try just about anything. My friend took me to her acupuncturist. The experience was of pain relief. I was fortunate enough to go another time before he moved to a location that was too difficult for me to get to. The second time, I actually felt the affected area of my brain as if it was knitting itself together.

I started to study and use trigger points, following the Bonnie Prudden method. Trigger points are found throughout the muscles of the body. When the climate is right the muscle goes into spasm and this causes pain. By following her technique, using a system mapping the trigger points of the body, it is possible to get pain relief without medication.

The method of shiatsu I was learning was called, Ohashiatsu. Its name is a combination of the name of the creator of this method, Ohashi, and shiatsu. The key word in this method is balance, referring to the physical and spiritual positioning of the practitioner while delivering the therapy. It is a holistic method. It is a method of caring and supporting. It is a system of mapping and using energy points. The central point of the mapping is around the abdominal area, called the Hara. Ohashi diagrams the Hara into 12 sections that correspond to the meridian for the heart, stomach, triple heater, lung, large intestine, small intestine, liver, gall bladder, heart constrictor, spleen, kidney, and bladder. By examining the Hara, a diagnosis can be made. Traditional shiatsu can be painful. In Ohashiatsu, there is no pain.

In Pilates, the exercise focus is on the core, the muscles of the abdomen, from which strength emanates. It uses a series of stretches to strengthen the body from the core out. The exercises are mainly floor exercises, which can be compared to ballet exercises, which emphasize the abdomen, but done in a standing position.

5-16-08

Yoga is a system of meditation through controlled breathing and exercises to strengthen and add flexibility to the body.

Yoga should be done with a sense of ease. There are several exercise programs on television. The one I like best is Yoga with Wai Lana on PBS (Public Broadcasting System). What I particularly like about her program is that while she is demonstrating each movement, she explains the benefits.

I have danced and studied various forms of dance all my life. Dance above all has given me a practical and intuitive knowledge of my own body. It strengthens me physically and spiritually. Different forms of dance are recognized by specific types of movement. Each brings strength and flexibility in its own way. Each one uses the abdomen as a center. Ballet is very linear as is tap and most ballroom dancing, with the exception of Latin dancing; in belly dancing the center of weight shifts with the hip. In belly dancing, jazz, and modern dance, the hip movement and isolation of all parts of the body play an important role.

      The Alexander Technique is a holistic approach that stresses alignment and balance. By applying these methods to activities of daily living and recreation, one can benefit greatly. Two examples are: 1.getting down to and up from a sitting position, 2. a golf swing. Frederick Alexander was a professional orator who recited speeches from Shakespeare. At one point in his career Mr. Alexander lost his voice and was unable to speak. His doctors had no hope for him. He believed he could find a way to reverse this problem.
With determination and persistence, he applied exercises to balance and align his head, neck, and spine. His voice was restored and he continued to recite from Shakespeare.

Exercise: Neck stretch
Start with the head center, eyes looking straight ahead, arms at the sides.
1. Turn head as far to the left as you can while breathing in to a count of four. Exhale to a count four while returning the head to center. Repeat to the right.
   Repeat exercise.
2. Extend the chin as if you are a turtle coming out of your shell. Inhale. Count four. Exhale. Count four as you return to center.
   Inhale. Extend the head back into your turtle shell touching the cervical spine. You will appear to have a double chin. Count four.
   Exhale. Count four as you return to center.
   Repeat exercise.
3. Head center. Eyes front. Inhale. Lower the ear toward the shoulder. Count four.
   Exhale. Count four as you return to center.
   Repeat on the other side.
   Repeat exercise. Note: You may feel the stretch all this way down to the fingers.
4. Inhale. Count four while you bow the head.
   Exhale. Count four while you return to center.
   Stand tall. Feel as though you are a marionette with the string lifting the top of your skull.
   Inhale. Slowly, while counting four, reach/stretch arms up, arms turned toward each other above your head. Feel very tall.
   Arch back, only to the level of the bottom of the shoulder blades.
   Feel the abdominal muscles working to support this position. Eyes look back at the ceiling towards the wall behind you. Feel the long neck. Lift your arms, reaching towards the wall behind you.
   Exhale. Count four as you return to center; use abdominal muscles to support the return to this position.
   Turn hands/palms away from your body and lower your arms gently to your sides.
   Exhale. Count four as you return to center; use abdominal muscles to support the return to this position.
   Turn hands/palms away from your body and lower your arms gently to your sides.

The links between all of these modalities are alignment, the abdomen, and balance.

CHAPTER 5 - Teaching dance

5-22-08

In the process of learning the different methods, I applied them personally to myself. There is a saying in dance when learning technique: first there is the knowing and then there is the doing. So I would look very carefully at the instructions and act upon them. In working with these therapies I would analyze and internalize and apply the instructions. Only after applying the technique could I realize what it really was. Slowly, I started to feel a little more confident. After only a year or so, I was able to walk without pain. On Shabbos I walked two blocks to my shul. After the service, people mill around visiting each other. I was speaking with one of the women. She was talking about the beautiful spring weather, soon to be summer, which brought thoughts of bathing suits and exercise. Knowing that I taught dance, she asked me if I would start a women's exercise class. Hmmmmm. Why not? My studio is available now. I just have to let the world know. Before I walked out of the shul, I had two more students, so that made three. I advertised this class as a combination of Pilates, yoga, and dance techniques. During that week I attended a shiur and had two more students. We started Thursday morning. Now I had a chance not only to exercise for myself, but also to have company and be able to teach the techniques that I had learned to others. And so started my adventure into teaching other women the things I had learned. I charged for the class but it was a suggested donation to the Bikur Cholim Organization, a Jewish community-supported charitable organization. This was my opportunity to give something back to the Bikur Cholim Organization, which had been so helpful to me at the beginning of my recovery. My *neshumah*, my soul, was healing along with my body.

When spring and summer were over and the high holidays approached, classes were suspended. When they resumed, some people who were snowbirds left for Florida; others had developed other interests. There was one person, and then another person joined. I taught even for the two. One of my former students, now an adult who had been a ballet student of mine as a child, asked me if I would teach a class at night. Why not? This developed into an evening class with several students. The more I worked with people, the more I healed.

CHAPTER 6 - Watching my granddaughter

5-23-08

My daughter started her prenatal massage business. She needed some help. She asked me if I would be able to watch my granddaughter Nadiva, two days a week. Her given name is Minerva Lily, Mina for short. I lovingly call her by her Hebrew name, Nadiva, which means noble and generous. I thank Mollie for having the confidence in me, for trusting me so soon after my hospitalization with her treasure. Of course I did baby-sit. It became a very long day for my daughter. She started out at her home in Bayonne, New Jersey and picked me up at my home in Far Rockaway at seven a.m. She would bring me back to Bayonne so I could watch Nadiva. Then she would go off to Hoboken to work. I stayed over the following day and came back that night.

It was my pleasure to watch my granddaughter while being able to help my family. I was able to watch Nadiva go through her milestones, her walking, her talking, her eating and toilet training. I read to her. In the process of reading to her I concentrated on trying to pronounce each syllable clearly so that I would hear and learn correctly. It was an enormous speech lesson for me. She was very patient with me. She understood that I was trying very intently. She was at the beginning independent walking stage. She was not used to walking distances. Half a block away and across the street, was a little children's park alongside the river; this was perfect for the two of us. It was a challenge for each of us in our own way, to walk from home to the playground. We shared many moments enjoying the playground. Nadiva was able to expand her skills and I was delighted to help her. When the weather was good we had picnics in the park. For a while, she was a very picky eater; however, when she was distracted with play in the park, she ate. Having other children in the park, though they were not directly sharing, provided a sense of being part of the group. As time progressed, she reached the level of being able to relate directly with another child to share play. It was a chance for me as well to have conversation with another adult. There was one mother and child we saw often at the park; the two children played very well together. We looked forward to seeing them and made play dates. A child's activities were a chance for a lot of physical activity for me; bending, stretching, walking, and lifting. I grew stronger. Nadiva grew stronger also. We were able to expand our horizons; we were able to walk further and further.

Walking, in addition to stimulating the areas of the feet with their numerous nerve endings, relates to all parts of the body. **The action of walking acts as a pump to circulate the blood, bringing nutrients and oxygen throughout the body.**

We were able to walk to the next part of the park along the river while we watched the bocce players. We were able to walk along the river while we watched the people fishing. We were able to walk back. It was a good match; her little legs and my slow speed of walking. When we walked in the other direction along the river, we came to another playground area with swings. It was a big treat for Nadiva to go to the swing park; she loved to swing. **My arms** were getting strengthened while pushing her.

Shoulder and arm exercise:
Place fingertips onto shoulders, elbows to the sides. (Starting position is called 'place '). Extend the arms out to the sides. Return to place. Extend arms to front. Return to place. Extend arms up. Return to place. Repeat exercise.

I made up little tunes, words to go with the activity of swinging. I started to teach her to pump herself. Over the course of time she got the hang of it and became a little more independent. She explored the big swings, which were low enough for her to climb on belly down, and push herself. With help she managed to find a way to get seated and pump herself.

5-25-08

Sundays were a stay-at-home day. I had requests to start a class for four, five, and six-year-olds. I taught them creative movement. It was a compliment to me to have this request come from two of my adult students, one of whom had been my student as a child. I believe that learning takes place when the student has fun. It was fun for me too. As time went by, my daughter requested that I stay over two additional days to help her expand her business, so I did. Nadiva celebrated her second birthday at the end of May. The spring weather was lovely. I took advantage of it. The rainbow sprinkler was turned on in the park. It was time for mainly outdoor play. It was time for running through the icy cold water of the sprinklers. Nadiva wouldn't do it without me doing it too. Spring went into summer. We took advantage of the town pool. There was a beautiful kiddy pool with sprinklers in the pool. One was a waterfall and one was a shower. They had a large regular pool. Of course, I wanted to get in there too, so I took Nadiva with me into the big pool. She clung to me. I walked across the pool with her; finally she was getting comfortable enough to loosen and eventually let go of her grip. She was strong. With good experiences, she felt secure. She was able to feel comfortable floating on my arm and turning on her stomach. What she liked best was to hold onto me when I tried to swim a little bit. This was really tough for me; the coordination to achieve this was very difficult and very exhausting, but also very satisfying. I extended the swimming lesson to bath time at home, where I was able to teach her to blow bubbles in the water. I think that people who have fear of the water may have never learned to put their heads under the water.

The fall came around and we celebrated my birthday. My sister Esther met us at the kosher deli in Staten Island and we had dinner.

CHAPTER 7 - Access-A-Ride

Because of my disabilities I applied for Access-A-Ride. I finally felt comfortable to have this source of semi-independence. I had to go through the application process. There were forms to be filled out. My daughter took a photo of me for the application. Off to the mail it went. About a month later I received an appointment for an interview with instructions to call for a car service to take me to the interview site at Kennedy Airport. The waiting room was filled with people waiting for a variety of city medical services. It was my turn. The interviewer came out to escort me down a long hallway to the interview room. I couldn't keep up with her. She was already down the end of the hallway while I was seemingly creeping along. She had a look of impatience on her face. She asked me about my history and my medications. I was thinking to myself, why all these questions when all this information was sent in the application? I couldn't remember the name of one of the medications. This one had a very difficult name to spell and pronounce. People who see the name of this medication usually fluster. It's called dipyridamole. There was a bus in the room. I was asked to board the bus. I did. I followed her instructions and took a seat. She asked me if I could see the destination sign. I did and then I exited. It was very difficult coming down the stairs. I lost my balance and caught myself on the railing, holding with two arms before falling. Then I sat down at the interview desk where I was told to fill out my name and address and sign the form. I had been practicing this skill. I was told that I would hear from them within three weeks with the results of the interview, if I would be accepted or not for Access-A-Ride service. My thoughts were negative. Okay, I could board the bus. What did I need "Access-A-Ride" for? I could see and read the sign. I could write my name and address. I had come a long way to do those things. Three weeks later I received the letter of acceptance. I was now able to travel throughout New York City's five boroughs. I was very happy.

Now, I was able to take Access-A-Ride to an address in Staten Island near the Bayonne Bridge, where my daughter could meet me, bring me to her home, and bring me back to the pickup point for the return trip home.

CHAPTER 8 - Certificate of Occupancy

5-26-08

Quarters became too tight. There was too much lack of privacy. As a result, my job taking care of Nadiva ended. Mollie continued to work. In these days, with our economic situation, most families are not able to make it on one income and Mollie's family was no exception. I missed the routine but soon filled my time with other things.

My house was under renovation from before I moved, in the late 1990's. When you start a project of this enormity, the inexperienced person has no clue what she is getting into. I lived a very simple lifestyle. There were no frills. My salary went to improving the house. The house had been built in 1920; it was constructed with the intent to last one hundred years. It aged and needed reconstructive surgery. The foundation was good but everything else needed help. After a time, I hired an architect so that I could make this into a two-family house with an office. This caused me an enormous amount of stress and aggravation. It had not been resolved before I got sick. After I returned from the hospital and was able to turn toward this matter, I found that I was unable to deal with it on my own. My son took over the quest. The architectural firm was devious, underhanded, and generally dishonest. My son stayed with it and over the next two years, was able to bring this to a conclusion. Thank God my house is now legalized. I get very inward when I think of the process that I had to go through. With the legalization of the house it is necessary to hire an architect or engineer to do this process. If you don't have an upstanding firm or architect to work for you, which unfortunately you can't know until you find out, you have a terrible mess on your hands, and you don't know it until it's too late. The legal avenues for help are not really sufficient. I contacted the Better Business Bureau and another legal board association. They were very sympathetic on the telephone but not very helpful in my situation. They would investigate, which would take at least six years. They would be happy to investigate, but they couldn't do anything for me to speed the process up, or to get financial restitution to me. All they could do basically was to give the architectural firm a slap on the wrist. I was not supposed to have the stress that this brought about. After the stroke, the pitch of my voice became very distinctive, to the point of being weird. When I called up the architectural firm they brushed me aside. They passed me from one person to another, ending with the expeditor. My sister Phillis suggested that I tape record my conversations with them; these tapes were very telling. The business manager was extremely rude and demanded more money than we had contracted for in the beginning; the architect had verbally promised me that he would be there with the inspector at the time of the inspection. Conveniently, he didn't remember. I had paid for the architect to make a final inspection.

The first time it was inspected it didn't pass. The inspector made a list of objections: 1.The architect's plan was not an accurate representation of the building. 2. Stairs and porch railings were not high enough according to the most recent building code. 3. One smoke detector was missing. 4. Leaders and gutters were needed.

The proper number of smoke detectors had already been installed, but was not noticed by the inspector. I added one more for good measure. The railings were grandfathered in. I immediately had leaders and gutters installed.

The expeditor told me that when the revisions were complete I should make an appointment for a new inspection.

5-27-08

I thought it was the expeditor's job to make the appointment, but I didn't quibble. I did it. The inspector came and said, "Where are the new plans?" I shrugged my shoulders, "what?" That was the second inspection. I was floored. The expeditor continued to give me misinformation. I was so close to getting what I needed to make my house a legal two-family house. I was hanging on. Again, I made another appointment. This time it took much longer to get the appointment. The appointment was made for the next month. The expeditor said that he would bring me the plans himself and be there before the inspector would get there. The inspector came but the expeditor didn't. I called the expeditor; he said he was on his way. The inspector could no longer wait. He was very nice and told me I could call his boss and if he had permission he would come back to my building later that day, provided I called that the plan was there. The inspector's boss gave the okay. The expeditor never came.

I called the architectural firm; the architect who made the plan was no longer with the firm. I was fortunate enough to speak with the head person, who told me that the plans were on his desk. He was going to do what was necessary without any charge. Of course, I thought I had already paid for the service; why should I have to pay additionally? This architect, the head of the firm, was the person who signed for all of the documents as the responsible party. The architect who was working directly with me told me in the beginning that the head of the firm had already received his cut in order to put his signature on the documents.

The head stated that, since there was no additional fee, he had at least thirty other clients to take care of first. I knew I was sunk. He said, "Well I'm telling you the truth, or would you rather deal with the expeditor (which meant continual lies)." I didn't know what to do. I couldn't handle it. I gave it completely to my son.

5-28-08

What a relief to have backup. My son dealt with their lies and divisiveness. Through my son's efforts, I received the updated plans. The inspector came. He was the same one who had made the previous visit and had tried to be helpful. He noticed that the architect's drawing (rendering) failed to reflect one of the windows. Everything else was in order. The inspector gave the building a passing mark. Thank God the Certificate of Occupancy (C. of O.) was recorded in the Building Department records, which can be accessed by computer. I made a copy. The architectural firm tried to withhold the document for ransom. Because of my son's diplomacy, I received the C. of O.

I had always thought, do what you can and God will help you with the rest. I had a bit of a wonder woman complex. But I gave that up many years ago when I was living in the Adirondacks. I even had a headscarf that reminded me of Wonder Woman's headband with its stripes and stars. My attitude changed. Now, whatever it is that has to be done, I do what I can do with God's help. God's help comes in many ways. God gave me my son as a helper. My son saw it through to completion. It had been a difficult and arduous process. It was a relief to hold the Certificate of Occupancy in my hand.

CHAPTER 9 - Spring 2008 Garden

Spring had come again. My thoughts turned toward my gardens. I had wintered over my geranium plants in the attic where they thrived in the sunny windows. They got so big that it became difficult to carry them down my circular winding staircase. I needed my son's aid again and somehow he was able to bring them down. My north porch was filled with flowers. It's my summer kitchen. I spend a lot of time enjoying being there. I also experimented with vegetable plants on the lawn. I cleared a small portion and planted green pepper and tomato plants. I have always enjoyed gardening and since my illness found it therapeutic. My vegetable yield was small but tasty. This year (spring 2008), I expanded my vegetable garden. It's still quite small; you can put a lot of plants into a small area. With God's help they will thrive.

CHAPTER 10 - Tevye the Milkman (a/k/a Fiddler on the Roof)

The administrator of the Shulamith Elementary School asked if I would help with the dance portion of their annual production. I was honored to be asked. They wanted to pay me. I would have done it gratis, but I don't believe in working without being paid. So I told the administrator that I would like instead to donate an amount to the Bikur Cholim. I know that the school can't afford a lot of money, so I told them to donate according to their means.

The sixth grade girls were putting on *Tevye the Milkman (a/k/a Fiddler on the Roof)*. I choreographed dances for them and taught them all the dances within six weeks. After spending only an hour or so twice a week, they were able to learn the steps. The last week I came in more often and stayed late. The girls were very excited and motivated to practice a lot on their own. It was exciting for me.

I was able to bring my three-and-a-half-year-old granddaughter with me to some of the practice sessions. The girls I was not directly working with were wonderful with her. They played together, so my granddaughter was happy to be there. This made it possible for me to work without interference from the other girls. The show was a success. The atmosphere was electrifying. The costumes, the lighting, the music, the makeup, and the sets; all these things helped make up the production. The actors were all in place for this one exciting night. It was theater.

CHAPTER 11 - The Amen Group

As a child of twelve years, I learned to write the Hebrew letters and even learned to read a little bit. I took a year of Hebrew language at college with the intent to read the prayers better. At the end, I could read the words better but I still did not have proper pronunciation or vocabulary. I would try to read the Hebrew and then the English translation so I would know what I was reading. Twenty-five years later, when I was in the hospital, I used the siddur that the rabbi gave me as my English textbook. It was very difficult for me to read the English at this point. The Hebrew was impossible.

During this past year I became acquainted with a group called The Amen Group. The group started a few years ago by women who were concerned about a neighbor's young daughter, Sarit, who was afflicted with cancer. They met in the basement of the family's house, where they would say prayers and answer Amen.

As told by Esther Stern in her book, "*Just one word. Amen*" *(2005)*, "The root of *emunah,* faith, is the word *Amen. Amen* is also an acronym of the three words *E-l Melech Ne'eman;* thus, when we say *Amen,* we are affirming our belief that Hashem (God) is a "faithful God and King."

We thank God throughout the day. As the spirit moves them, individuals in the group stand and recite a series of fourteen blessings thanking God. After hearing each blessing, the group responds, "Amen". The series is repeated till at least 100 blessings have been said. Psalms of David are said in unison. Someone presents a small topic of learning. Throughout, there is sharing of various joyous and sad happenings in people's lives. Then we go on to our individual prayers.

Unfortunately Sarit did not survive, but the group has. It has grown exponentially to over 100 women. Six days a week, it has become a place of prayer, learning, and support.

Through my association with the Amen Group I became motivated to tackle recognition of the Hebrew letters, to read Hebrew words, and eventually read the text with understanding. Slowly, slowly, slowly, I hope one day to read the prayers at a normal speed and with understanding. My next door neighbor listened to me recite the words, to help me learn the correct pronunciations. Each letter with its corresponding vowel is enunciated. She has great patience. I would vocalize these strange sounds over and over and over, until I was satisfied that they resembled a word. It didn't take long before the sound became familiar. I am still dreadfully slow; I need lots of practice, lots of repetitions.

CHAPTER 12 - Physical progress

This year my body has been getting stronger and my alignment is still in the process of correction. It is so much better than from the time of the last MRI of my spine. I'm able to walk without pain, as long as I don't overdo it, and always, always am aware of my alignment.

My peripheral eyesight has improved. When I was in the hospital I had no peripheral vision on my right side. I was actually blind on the right periphery. I was seen by a specialist in the hospital, a neurologist of the eye. He gave me a lengthy examination and concluded that I would have no peripheral vision. He had a student with him. She continued to look and noticed one minuscule area that could lead to vision. I could have the peripheral vision restored in time. I don't know how the process works, that one tiny spot can be instrumental in waking up a whole system. I'm so pleased to have the potential for normal vision and I thank God for that. To begin with, I was physically unable to read. Then I was unable to read for any length of time. Reading itself was very slow while combining sight, sound, and meaning in my head. I wasn't disturbed by this arduous process. I knew that progress comes in very, very small increments. At this point, three years later, I am not really up to speed but I am enjoying my reading. I have read several books on health topics and have recently finished a lengthy novel, which I enjoyed very much. I enjoyed stories and had listened to books on tape, and now found that there is no comparison to the joy of truly reading.

Eye Exercise 1:

Scrunch the eyes. Release.   Repeat 3 times.

Life Extension Magazine January 2009 report, "Relieve Your Tired Eyes While Guarding Against Common Eye Diseases" by Laurie Barclay, MD: *"Lactic-acid build-up in muscles, which normally contributes to exercise-related muscle cramps and fatigue…"*

The intrinsic muscles of the eye serve to focus the eye and control the amount of light entering it. The 6 extrinsic eye muscles control the eye's movement to the sides, up and down, and clockwise or counter clockwise all the way around.

When using the following exercises, the motion of the eyes act as windshield wipers, clearing the lactic acid.

Eye Exercise 2:
Hold your arms and hands straight to your sides to the extremes of your peripheral vision.
Look straight ahead. Without moving the head, using ONLY the eyes, look to the left hand, then center, and then to the right hand, and back to center. Repeat.
Change your arm and hand positions.
Reach the left arm and hand up and to the side. Reach the right arm and hand down and to the side. Check that both hands are in the extremes of your peripheral vision. With your eyes ONLY, look up to the left hand, center, down, and center. Repeat.
Reverse hand positions and repeat exercise.

Make clockwise circles with eyes. Look up, right side, down, and left. Repeat.
Repeat the above making counter clockwise circles.
Reach arm in front, palm facing up. Look into the palm. Look into the distance. Repeat 3 times.
Close your eyes for a few seconds. Open them up and feel refreshed.

6-2-08

The right side of my body was affected by the stroke. My right hand started out with absolutely no feeling after the stroke. That was my dominant hand. Two and a half years ago, when I first got the gift of the computer, I had to learn every aspect of its basic use again. There was no control with my right hand. It was as if my right hand was a separate entity.

The return of fine motor coordination has been making progress over the last two and a half years. I still have to look at my hand in order to insure that it is placed correctly on the keyboard. Before, my hand would go where it wanted without asking me and I would have to find it and replace it. It became a losing game. Now I am starting to gain some control. I find that I have more control of my thumb and index finger than the rest of my fingers when it comes to placement on the keyboard. Perhaps this is not really control, but the middle, ring, and pinky fingers need to do more stretching.

> **Finger Stretching Exercise:**
>
> 1. Make a fist and then release each finger separately and stretch that finger without moving the others. The stretched finger remains in its last position, the stretched or extended position, while continuing to stretch the subsequent fingers.
> 2. The thumb stretches back toward the palm. The other four fingers remain extended. The index finger stretches to the palm. This procedure is repeated with the remaining fingers bringing all the fingers to the closed position.
> 3. The first part is repeated, but starting with the closed fist and reaching and extending the pinky.
> 4. Repeat part two, except the pinky leads the way.

I learned this exercise from my daughter when she was very involved with juggling many years ago. I have had many instances to practice it as a fine motor coordination exercise for dance and relaxation. Try it. It's one of those exercises that sound simple enough, but when you do it you find how complex it really is.

Another exercise I find helpful.

> **Finger Stretching Exercise 2:**
>
> Have the fingers extended and then reach the index finger to the thumb and touch the tips of them both together, and then bring the index back to the original position. The same procedure is repeated on all the other fingers as well.

At first it was difficult to do all these exercises; now I have much more facility. These exercises are also very good for in focusing. It's impossible to do these exercises without focusing intently on them.

CHAPTER 13 - Health insurance and treatment

6-3-08

In the years that I worked for the school system I had what was considered very good health coverage. I had GHI and Empire Blue Cross for my hospital coverage. I also had a separate plan provided by the union, for dental coverage. These were all paid provisions of the union contract. I purchased an additional rider for major medical, which was very nominally priced. It came to just a few dollars a month. I was very happy to not have to use my coverage very often. It was primarily used for yearly checkups. I was very fortunate to have it when I got my major illness.

My hospitalization was covered. I didn't understand until this period of my life that coverage for the doctors and the hospital were separate issues. The doctors were covered by GHI for the most part. My care was so extensive that I had to pay the additional amounts on my own. While I was in the hospital I had no thoughts of my financial obligations. My only thoughts were to get well again. When I got home, that was a different story. Although Michael took care of my bookkeeping, as I was incapable of physically writing the checks, I was very much aware of my bills. The hospital got paid directly from Empire Blue Cross during that time. That was very good for me. The system of payment from GHI was different. The doctors submitted their bills, and GHI sent the payment to me with their explanation. The payment then had to be sent to the doctors. At times, when there were multiple doctors in a group, the doctors would send different bills and the distribution of payment would be confusing.

I had a stack of bills two inches high. That's a lot of bills. It seemed that every single person who glanced at me sent a bill. Keeping track of everything was indeed a job. It's very easy to let the papers get out of hand. I had an oversized loose-leaf notebook from my schoolwork. I dumped everything out and started to put some order into the bills. I put little "stickups" as dividers to indicate each doctor's account. This made it much easier to locate and coordinate statements from the doctors and payments from the insurance companies.

In the first hospital, the emergency room, a doctor assigned to me without my permission was not covered by my insurance. The ambulance attendants had all my insurance information, so there was no reason I should have had a doctor not covered by my plan. After I started receiving bills from the emergency room doctor, I called up the hospital to see what the problem was. They told me now that they had recently changed to a different billing format; that the emergency room came under one kind of coverage, and the doctor under another. I called up GHI to find more about this and indeed there was a new ruling that the doctors could bill "if they wished" as a separate coverage. It still didn't give the emergency room the right to give me a doctor not in my plan. They had enough staff to give me proper care with someone who did participate in my coverage.

6-4-08

On my sixty-fifth birthday I reached the age of Medicare entitlement. What a relief. I thought my future medical bills would be covered. Some doctors do not accept Medicare payment. In this situation I have to pay the doctor and then apply to Medicare for reimbursement. GHI is my secondary insurer; my understanding is that whatever Medicare does not cover is picked up by GHI. When I worked I had a very small deductible and my insurance was paid for through union contract with a small payment for additional coverage. With Medicare I have a deductible. With GHI I also have a deductible. I pay much more now for my premiums, both for Medicare and GHI. My Medicare premium is automatically deducted every month from my social security check. The GHI premium is deducted monthly from my very small pension check. I thought Medicare would cover my medical expenses, so the year before being eligible for Medicare I didn't go for frequent checkups. My doctor wanted me to go at least once every quarter. I felt that I couldn't afford this luxury. I thought I'd wait until Medicare kicked in. I waited till one year passed since my last doctor's appointment, and felt it was very important to have a checkup whether I had to pay up front or not. Dr. Smiles was very good about taking care of my prescriptions and overseeing my health tests, even though I hadn't visited him all year. I made an appointment. Dr. Smiles was pleased with my progress. I didn't feel comfortable with my finances and medical coverage at this point. I started to feel very low and edgy. I communicated my concern with Dr. Smiles. He saw that my blood work showed that I was anemic. He sent me for a consultation with a hematologist. After two visits with the hematologist, he concurred I had anemia. He sent me for further tests to find the origin of the problem, or at least to narrow the cause of the problem with a gastroenterologist. I made an appointment with a gastroenterologist for a colonoscopy and a gastroscopy. If all went well then they could give me both tests, one after the other. In order to take this test you have to make preparations. The doctor told me to have no food for twenty-four hours prior to the test. He gave me a prescription for a kind of salt and a flavoring packet, to be mixed in a gallon of water, to be consumed in a six hour period at a rate of eight ounces every ten minutes prior to the test. The last thing I ate was a bowl of oatmeal with flax seeds. I'm a woman with a small frame. Drinking one gallon of water within the prescribed time was not happening. I downed three quarters of it and called it quits. Unfortunately, that was not enough to wash out the flax seeds. Consequently, the test was a wash and the second test was aborted. I still don't know the cause of my anemia. It's really difficult to get the right balance for nutritional intake. If you eat meat and dairy products there will be a danger of elevating cholesterol. On the other hand, if you depend on legumes and vegetables it is difficult to satisfy your nutritional needs.

PART THREE

SUMMING UP   2-13-13

It is February 13, 2013. I just finished rereading what I had written about my recovery during the period from April 2005 to June 2008. It's time to go on.

My body has become stronger. I have gained much more feeling on my right side, the side corresponding to the left brain stroke. I haven't taken steroids for several years. My face no longer looks like a ripe pumpkin and I am wearing my size 4 and size 6 skirts. I am down to two different medications and vitamins each day. They are dipyridamole, aspirin, calcium citrate, and B-complex. The dipyridamole needs to be taken three times daily with no food for two hours before and one hour after. How's that for a diet plan! When I eat, I eat my meals and snacks with gusto and thankfulness.

Of course, I am continuing to write my saga. My eye/hand coordination is getting better. I still have to look at the keyboard, but I recognize each letter and know where each key is. I still have to encourage my right hand to maintain its proper place on the keyboard. My spelling has improved a little, but thank God for spell check. When the computer doesn't recognize a word, I try to work out the puzzle. Sometimes the orders of the letters or the syllables need to be changed, or there may be too many extraneous letters. Even if none of the spell check choices are a match, they give me clues to look at the puzzle in a different way. Eventually, ah ha!

I went to visit the sick at Peninsula Hospital today. My friend Sarah has asked me many times to go with her. Up till now, I was not capable psychologically. Now I was able to handle it and use some counseling skills. Many years before, I had been the social worker in a local nursing home. Twice I went with Sarah to visit the sick through the Bikur Cholim Organization. The first time I was pleased that I could help to give the patients some support. The second time I enjoyed giving the patients support, but I could not take the smell of urine and illness. I became afraid for my own health. Peninsula Hospital has since closed.

The economy had gotten difficult. Wherever I have lived, the walls expanded to accommodate the needs of my family. Thus in December 2007, my daughter, son-in-law, and granddaughter came to share my home. The walls expanded again as we excitedly celebrated the birth of a new granddaughter. The midwife put her in my arms. What a beautiful feeling to connect to a new life.

As the days went on, the parents worked. The children spent their time in school, day care, and Grandma Care. God gave me strength. Caring for my grandchildren was a joy as well as a mental and physical workout. We were very involved with a slew of activities: reading, schoolwork, religious observance, Hebrew, artwork, dancing, playground activities, swimming, walking, skating, going out for pizza, going to the library, and visiting friends. Each of these activities helped me grow. Statistically, how does one keep two little girls who are four years apart, gainfully and peacefully occupied? When I worked in counseling middle school youngsters, my basic teaching plan revolved around four key words: *FOCUS, RELAX, RESPECT, and RESPONSIBILITY*. I should have added *PATIENCE*. The students and I were interactive. For example, I composed a rap song: *Do what you do when you're doin' it.* The students made the second line. *You jump when you jump, you walk when you walk. You do what you do when you're doin' it.* The students "sang" their rap. Some got up and demonstrated their rap. Nothing is learned without fun, enjoyment and a sense of accomplishment, no matter how small.

So what did I learn from this? If I have a relaxed demeanor, focus on the task at hand, take my responsibility seriously, respect my limitations, be patient and loving, the girls will do well. Consequently, we learned and we usually had fun.

After three years it was time for my family to move on to their own home.

How am I? Of course I miss them and their constant activity. Life goes on and there is so much to do. When people say "I'm bored", I retort, "being bored, no; only boring people".

God keeps us on our toes.

We have been having very erratic weather. Hurricane Sandy in November 2012 left severe damage in its wake. Houses not far from mine suffered flood damage. My friend's basement was flooded, effecting the floor, walls, appliances, heating system, plumbing, and wiring. My house is on higher ground. Thank God, I only had wind damage, blowing roof shingles off. I was left without heat and electricity for two weeks. It was too cold to stay home without heat. I stayed for the first week. My neighbor was evacuating to a friend in Brooklyn and gave me a ride to my sister. She was preparing for a move to another apartment. There were boxes all over. It didn't matter. I was happy to be with my sister. She has custody of my niece's hound dog named Willow. She is sweet, smart, and affectionate. She reminded me of the storybook character *Clifford*. I grew fond of her and enjoyed taking her for walks.

The presidential election was held in spite of the disaster. I found out that the specific date could not be changed, as it was specified in the constitution. Allowances were made for displaced persons. I voted in Brooklyn for the president, but was unable to vote for candidates in my local district. The library in Brooklyn was accommodating. They issued me a library card which gave me access to their computers. Most of us in my neighborhood became Hurricane Sandy refugees. Some were only able to return to their homes in February 2013. This is February. Two years ago at this time, it was 50 degrees. This morning it was 17 degrees.

On and off I have been steadily practicing the violin. I am amazed and thankful to God for the ability to connect dots, to form new neural pathways. Little by little, with each small increment, my fingers, arms, and vision have become more accurate in producing recognizable and pleasing sounds. Playing the violin is a source of physical, mental, and spiritual satisfaction. Being able to connect the dots, the musical notations, means to read with understanding, to give it life. It is a source of solace for me, a positive escape from the mundane and worrisome. It is one of the ways to connect to spirituality. It is a source of joy. Even when I'm practicing and repeating and repeating and repeating and repeating a phrase and hating having to repeat it to make some progress, I love that I am able to stick with it, to focus, and make some progress. It's almost like a conquest.

Music is a language. It is a voice that stirs the intellect and emotions. At the beginning of my musical voyage with the violin, my abilities: my cognition, vision, hearing, speech, and tactile senses were completely disconnected. All these senses came together through learning to play the violin. As an added bonus, my ability to focus and my reading speed increased. Music is a language. It is a voice that stirs the intellect and the emotions. My goal when I play the violin is to be part of the instrument, whether I make up my own sounds or someone else's compositions; to make poetry through music.

When I was in high school I read a book called "The Poetics of Music" by the Russian composer, Igor Stravinsky (composer of *The Rite of Spring)*. It made a lasting impression on me. It was about the relationship of music to mathematics, form, structure, and emotion. It brings to mind Hebrew. The Hebrew language is the only language that correlates musical notation called trope, and the alphabetical and numerological systems to derive spiritual meanings. I think we are all looking for that balance of harmony in body, mind, and spirit to give us peace.

The National Grid gas workers were doing some planning outside my house. Of course I was curious. They told me that due to the hurricane, water pipes would be replaced. In order to do that, the gas line had to moved and then replaced. They came back with a contracted crew and heavy equipment and proceeded to dig up my sidewalk. It was noisy and dirty. It was difficult to exit and enter my house. The workers were polite to me, but inconsiderate when it came to my property. This past summer I had a sprinkler system put in and invested in a new perennial garden with many beautiful flowers. They scooped out the dirt from below the sidewalk and dumped it right on top of my new sprinkler system and my newly planted garden. I was fuming. When they were done they scooped off the dirt. I will see what the damage is this spring.

2-26-13

One day it's freezing, and the next day it's like spring. Even though there's a month more of winter, I'm starting to think about spring. It would be nice to plant blueberry bushes somewhere in my backyard. They require acidic soil. I bought a garden tool to indicate the acidity of the soil. This would guide me to give the plants a healthy environment. When planting edibles, there are bonuses. First, a lovely flower appears, then the colorful, shapely fruit or vegetable with its particular fragrance and fresh taste. No store bought produce can match the quality of homegrown, fresh-picked vegetables. Tending the garden is a healthy outdoor exercise. It's a chance to commune with nature and thank God for being part of the process.

I rediscovered the Roy Wilkins Park. In the days before I became ill, two days a week I counseled teens who were not doing well in the traditional school setting. *The Last Chance* class met at the Roy Wilkins Recreation Center, Jamaica, Queens. Their classrooms were in a bunker that former students had rebuilt. These students were intelligent, but needed a way to approach learning and improve their self-esteem. Together, through games and the arts, they learned the process of focusing, patience, politeness, relaxation, respect, responsibility, and decision making. They were fun to work with. As an added perk, I used the center's pool.

I greatly enjoy swimming. When I was really in shape, I could swim a mile. That's about 70.4 laps in a 75 foot pool. I've got a long way to go to get back to that. Swimming is a great exercise. Long ago, I worked out a swimming routine to stretch, strengthen, and relax my muscles and my mind. I find that if you change your stroke every lap, thus using different muscle groups, the muscles that were used have a brief rest. By doing this, I don't tire so soon. Consequently, I am able to do more than if I had used only one stroke. My pattern is: forward crawl, elementary back stroke, breast stroke, breast stroke on my back, side stroke on my left side, and side stroke on my right side. When swimming laps, it is difficult not to focus on that task. You forget about everything and let your mind rest.

When I was able to drive, I used to swim at the Long Beach Pool. Now that I don't drive it's difficult to get there. The Roy Wilkins Recreation Center pool had been under renovation and is now open again. With Access-A-Ride, I can take advantage of the facility. The water is warm and the other swimmers are polite. I bought a combination lock for the locker room. I memorized the combination. I practiced the combination, successfully opening and closing the lock several times. The next morning the Access-A-Ride picked me up and brought me to the pool. I stretched as I swam. I felt so good. I showered, dressed, and went to the locker to take out my pocketbook. I remembered the combination, but it wasn't opening. I tried again and again and again. Other ladies tried to help. Maybe I had the wrong order. No luck. I alerted the receptionist at the front deck and asked if someone could cut the lock. The park attendant was found and he located the cutter. He was ready to do the job only after all the ladies had exited from the locker room. Meanwhile, the Access-A-Ride was outside waiting for me. I ran outside and explained there was an emergency and to please wait for me. As other ladies exited the building, they stopped to chat with the driver and explain the situation. I am sure that helped. The Access-A-Ride rules allow for the driver to be up to 30 minutes late; however, the driver is not obligated to wait past 5 minutes for the rider. The last lady left the locker room. The park attendant came in and strained as he put pressure on the lock cutter and snapped the lock. We both sighed. I thanked him and ran out and hoped the driver was still there. He was. I thanked him and I thanked God. When I got home I checked the combination numbers. I did remember it correctly. I must have done something else wrong in the sequence. Anyway, no more combination locks.

2-28-13

Fall and winter passed along with some very dear loved ones.

5-12-13

Happily, life continues.

It's spring and, true to the song, April showers have brought May flowers. The lilacs perfume the air in my garden. All the perennial plants are budding; the hydrangeas, roses, lilies, gladiolas, azaleas, blue balloons, phlox and sedum, along with assorted herbs. Most of the plants that had been covered by dirt from below the sidewalk and dumped on top of my newly planted garden survived. I showed the crew photos of the damage. The contracted crew acted responsibly and had their landscapers replace the destroyed plants with my choice of new ones. The crepe myrtle tree that I had planted last fall is leafing out. The strawberries have lovely white flowers, promising fine fresh fruits. This spring's new additions are an apricot tree and three new blueberry bushes. The vegetable garden will soon be planted.

I take great joy in learning and using my experience, helping people, and helping my garden grow. May God continue to bless me with a positive outlook, and strength of body, mind, and soul, to always reach towards clarity and joy!

Perspectives of Family Members and Friends

Michael Rawitz

It started in 2005. It was Passover and I had gone away for the weekend to a friend's house for a Seder in upstate New York. There was no cell phone reception at my friend's house. On the way home I checked my cell phone; there was reception, and there also were twelve messages. I immediately knew that something was very wrong. My stomach sank; I felt sick. I started to listen to the messages and found out that my mom was in the hospital. The entire way back, I could not think of anything else and was terribly upset. I knew I couldn't do anything until I returned and got to my own car back on Long Island. I would then drive to Peninsula Hospital in Far Rockaway, Queens. When I arrived, she was in a hospital bed and struggling and screaming to get up. The hospital staff would not let her up and were trying to hold her down. They asked me to help hold her down. This was an extremely difficult thing for me to do or to watch. The doctors told our family that we should get our mom out of there and into another hospital. None of the doctors seemed to know what was wrong with her, what caused her stroke, or even if it was a stroke! They were not really calling it a stroke at that time. They put her in the traumatic brain injury area and held her there while they scheduled appointments for tests that were not going to occur for weeks. We wanted to get her out of that hospital, but they were giving us a hard time about releasing her. It was a terrible experience. After several days, my mom's sister Esther (my aunt) decided that she was going to take my mom out of this hospital and bring her to Manhattan to NYU, where she felt and we all felt she would get better care. Esther ordered a taxi to pick her up at Peninsula Hospital and bring them to NYU Hospital in New York City. Once she was there, my mom was assigned, supposedly, to the best doctor for her condition. The doctor was very pompous and in a rush, because he was on his way to Paris for the weekend. He told my mom to take some aspirin and wear sunglasses; nothing was wrong with her, and she would be released. We were shocked by his rash diagnosis, and then requested a new doctor. The new doctor was very good; he ordered tests, and received the test results within a day or so. One of the procedures ordered was an angiogram of the brain, which is a very invasive procedure. Unfortunately, while on the operating table, in the middle of the procedure, a blood clot loosened and traveled up to my mom's brain. She ended up having a stroke right on the operating table. This was horrible, but at the same time if it was going to happen this was probably the best place for her to be. Even knowing that a stroke is a possible risk during this procedure, the doctor who ordered the angiogram felt very responsible and he took extra special care of my mom. At this point my brother from Sweden, my sister from Canada, and my sister from New Jersey came to the hospital. I was at work when I found out about the stroke. I completely lost it at my office and told everyone that I was leaving. I went to get my car from the parking lot, but I was shaking so bad that I felt like I could not operate my car. I had to call my girlfriend to come pick me up and bring me to the hospital. After suffering this major stroke, my mom was paralyzed on the right side of her body and she lost the ability to speak. We were all very worried and scared. We called a family meeting at my aunt's apartment in Brooklyn and discussed the different possibilities that we might need to face in the future to care for my mother. We didn't know if she would need around the clock care. We didn't know if we could afford round the clock care. We didn't know if we would have to take turns caring for her. All these things were running through our minds as we discussed what was going to happen. The diagnosis after the stroke, CAT scans, and MRIs determined it to be a condition called primary vasculitis of the central nervous system. It happens when the blood vessels (for some unknown reason) become inflamed and constrict the flow of blood and oxygen to the brain. The treatment for this was going to be chemotherapy (similar to that of cancer patients). It was a toxic procedure, but it was a better alternative than the exploratory surgery that they wanted to perform, which we decided against. My older sister Dianna stayed with her overnight during this treatment to keep her company and help her. Mom was still unable to speak, but we were still somehow able to communicate by expressions and body language. After treatment, my mom remained at NYU for follow-up and physical therapy. It was several weeks and I remember driving to the hospital every weekend from Long Island to visit with mom to check on her progress. I would take her to an outside garden on the hospital grounds, where I would practice speaking with her and practice Kung Fu techniques to help with coordination. She would have to relearn how to use her muscles and her brain to do simple things that we take for granted that include: moving, writing, speaking, and communication; they were all extremely difficult for her. She still could not recall words and I could see in her face that she knew what she wanted to say, but could not make the connection in her brain for the word to come out of her mouth. After visiting her on the weekends, I would go back to her house, clean the property, and check all the bills. The bills were escalating (especially the medical bills). There were thousands and thousands of dollars in bills. I had to build spreadsheets to keep track of all the bills coming in, and the insurance payments, match them and make the payments, and keep track of the balance. It was an arduous task, but luckily I was able to keep track and get it done. While working in the yard many people stopped and asked about my mother. The community where she lives is a close knit one and a lot of people were praying for her. After several weeks of physical therapy, mom made amazing progress and was able to walk again. She still did not have feeling in most of her right side, but was able to walk slightly. Her speech was still impaired, but was improving. She practiced reading, speaking, and writing. Her writing before the stroke was very neat and stylish. After the stroke, her writing looked like that of a first grader learning how to write for the first time. The doctor advised that the first six months were critical, because that's when the majority of recovery takes place. There was a ton of medication that she needed to take. There were different doses at different times of the day; some had to be taken with food and some without food; it was very difficult to decipher, but it needed to be organized. I plotted a schedule according to all the different criteria and variables with the medication so that it would be safe for her to keep track of what to take and when. As the days and months progressed, my mom received more physical therapy and learned to speak and write again. We realized that Mom would never be able to drive a car again. She was too afraid. Her handwriting and speaking improved, but she never fully recovered and still retained a slight speech impediment. The speech impediment sounds perhaps like she has an accent and comes from a foreign country. The stroke aged her quite a bit. When looking at a picture prior to the event, compared to a picture taken afterwards, it is interesting to see that as the time progressed and she stopped taking some of the medicine (like the prednisone), she started to look better and better. It was quite a scary time for my family, which has a tumultuous history and relationship. It brought us together for my mom, but not completely. My mom brought us up as reform/conservative Jews, but as she aged she became an Orthodox Jew and expected her grown children to adopt her new ideology. We were already set in our ways and convictions and this caused a lot of tension and friction between us and our mom. This applied more to my sisters than my brother and me. I tried to explain to my mother that religion is a good thing when it brings people together, but when it starts to divide people then it is no longer a good thing. I consider myself a Jew; not an observant one and not an Orthodox one, but one who respects other people and feels for other people. To me, in my heart that is what I believe is the essence of Judaism. When a grandmother cannot see her grandchild on Saturday because she cannot travel or cannot talk to her on the phone because it's Shabbat it makes me sad, but this is the choice that my mom has made and we must live with her decision, even though that does not make it any easier. I am very happy that she has embraced our culture, but I wish she would be less imposing of her strict Orthodox values and a little more tolerant of others. Anyway, my mom recovered to the point where she was able to live in her house without assistance. She became stronger and was able to carry on with her life. She had to retire from her position as a guidance counselor before reaching retirement age, which placed her in a position to receive only a portion of her retirement. This was a tough blow to her income, but there was no choice. She was not in any condition to return to work and probably never would be again. I love my mother very much and I wish her the best of luck on this book. She is a strong-willed person and seems to be able to accomplish whatever she sets out to do. She has always been there for all her children and would do anything for us to help us out. I am eternally grateful!

Lila Baida

Sharon, I have known you for many years from the time before your crisis, hospitalization and post recovery.

The determination you had and still have, to overcome all these challenges, is enviable. You are a role model for me and many people coping with their own challenges and problems in life.

Mike Barnett

When you came home your speech sounded funny; you had trouble using a knife, scissors, and writing utensils, and walked slowly.

Not sure when, but about a year later I told you that you sound like Sharon again. *It seems you have no trouble cutting, writing, dancing, fixing furniture, walking, etc.*

How many people our age (or any age) can get up real early, walk .6 of a mile to the beach, swim and walk on the beach and walk .6 mile back home, climb your steps, and then think about having something to eat.

I get a tired feeling just thinking about trying to do this.

Faya Cohen

We knew Sharon from the Young Israel of Far Rockaway. That year we invited her for the second Seder (Passover Meal). The second night all was ready, but we were waiting for Sharon. Finally, I went to her house a few blocks away, and banged on the door. No answer. I did not know who else to ask about her whereabouts, and just had to hope that she was okay. Next day I found out what had happened the previous night.

Sometime later, I was with a mutual friend (Rochel obm) in the city, following an appointment with her doctor. Although we weren't sure about the timing, we were able to find parking near the hospital, so Rochel insisted that we go visit Sharon. We found her standing in her room with a smile, but not able to communicate very well. She was clearly very pleased to see us. We stayed a while, and left her to get back to her therapy.

Happily, I have kept up my friendship with Sharon over these years. She has been to our home for many Shabbos and holiday meals. We meet at different classes, and speak in between. I find her to be an amazing person, and a source of inspiration to me and to many other mutual friends and acquaintances.

The progress she has made since her sickness is nothing short of miraculous. She is clear proof that if you set your mind to doing something, with God's help, you can do anything. You just need to do the work. Work she did, and continues to do.

Sharon's speech has improved dramatically. Every now and then she still struggles to get a word out. It's like she's telling her brain it better cooperate or else. Eventually the word comes, her sense of humor intact.

Years after Sharon got sick, she broke her arm and did the required therapy. True to form, Sharon added her own therapy. She took out her old violin and told herself that she would play again. The violin is clearly not an instrument that one just picks up and starts to play. A beginner often spends months just learning to hold the instrument, before he or she begin to even play a note. Most wouldn't bother under the circumstances. Picking it up was not simple, for either hand. Positioning has to be just so. Sharon persisted, for weeks and months. She now has a certain comfort level of being able to play beginning tunes. She is on a path.

Gardening is another love of Sharon's. She is so happy to dig in the dirt to plant or pluck a wonderful vegetable or flower that she helped create. She is always encouraging others to do the same.

To sum it up, Sharon has been very blessed, and is to be commended for recognizing and appreciating her blessings. She is always trying to improve and learn more in so many areas, and encourages people around her to do the same. Life is never dull for her. God should help her continue in her path, and find happiness in every area of her life.

Lori Marton

I would like to share some thoughts regarding my dear friend Sharon. I met Sharon some years ago and she always struck me as a very intelligent, health conscious person. She walked with a very straight, erect stature that is commonly seen in trained dancers or yoga practitioners. She walks with grace.

I was very surprised to learn that she had been very ill and debilitated, since when I had met her she looked like the picture of health. I noticed that she spoke slowly and I thought that perhaps English was a second language for her, even though she had no accent. I suppose at that time English was a new language for her as she had to relearn so much after the illness. As I learned more about what she went through, I could not believe how devastating her illness was and yet what a miraculous and successful recovery Sharon has had. She not only has a command of the English language, speaking clearly and coherently, but she also has learned to read Hebrew and say the Jewish prayers in the original Hebrew. When we had opportunities to talk about what she had gone through, I was very impressed by her resilience, perseverance, and determination to bring herself back to be the best Sharon she can be. She is inspiring in how very disciplined she is with her diet and exercise.

I was fascinated by the stories she told me about her experience in the hospital. Getting inside the mind of a sick person who is non-communicative is very rare. I never heard from anyone what it is like to be locked in your own brain. These insights are so valuable and can be very effective in letting doctors, nurses, and visitors better understand the mind and needs of such patients. I have no doubt that Sharon's writings will be a great resource for so many. I wish her continued years of good health and may she be a great inspiration to many.

Pamela Eckhaus

I was asked to write about a woman that I have known for over fifteen years. This woman is a very special lady.

Sharon has been an important part of my life. She has always taught me to believe in myself and that I will succeed. Back in the day, before she had her battle with illness, she was a woman with black curly hair who appeared as an intellectual, sophisticated lady. She was a woman who was knowledgeable, a person I felt comfortable to speak to in my time of challenges. She also had the right things to say, which allowed me to have clarity in my own world of problems. She was a woman who had a smile on her face, always there, extending herself to help others.

After her illness struck, I didn't see her for a long time. I wondered how she was doing. I had heard she was very sick, but sadly I could do nothing but pray for her speedy recovery. "Thank you God for hearing my prayers and bringing Sharon back to us." But something was different. She now had gray hair and she was unable to communicate the way I remember. I wondered, will she ever be the Sharon I remember? Sharon in my eyes is a woman of valor. A woman of valor changes the world with her strength, her actions, and her good deeds.

Sharon needed to get better and she did. She had had the strength to learn all that had come easily but now was difficult. It was a challenge, but she overcame it. Her actions of helping others while she was battling her own obstacles waere shown throughout her recovery. Her good deeds shone like a bright light when she attended the Amen davening (prayer) group. She would not only pray for herself; she would pray for others as well. I know that for a fact because whenever I had a problem it would go away after speaking to her.

Sharon changed my world; she was and still is an inspiration and a great role model. She made my dreams come true by making me believe in myself. Her valor is golden; she stands up to the challenge no matter what.

Sharon, I wish you much success in your life endeavors. May you merit to see nachas (happiness) from your book. May we share in many simchas (joyous occasions) and may we both be worthy to see the coming of moshiach (the redeemer).

I LOVE YOU!!!!! Pamela Eckhaus

Sybil Sidelman Ryan

Caring for a teenager in the early 1980's, I was on duty in the ICU when his mother came to see him for the first time since being admitted after a motorcycle accident. She had been traveling from some distance away and I remember the staff looking at her and then each other with the same thought we later verbalized - "that's his mother?". Slim and youthful, she could have easily passed for his sister. Sharon and I became close friends after Eddie's discharge and that relationship continues to this day. I learned she was a dancer (and certainly looked the part) and someone who took a serious interest in health and wellness.

In 2005 Sharon was suddenly struck with a serious illness that resulted in a devastating stroke. She was in her early 60's and the severity of the event could have spelled the end of any sort of active life for most people, but Sharon isn't 'most people'. While still hospitalized she was asked by the physical therapist to set some goals for whatever recovery she might be able to achieve. When asked what she would like to be able to do, she had a simple one word answer: 'everything'; and then proceeded to accomplish just that. She regained full physical ability and speech, albeit with a subtle, interesting and unidentifiable 'foreign' accent. Charming.

Sharon has resumed teaching and is sharing her experience and knowledge in a 'how-to book' which is realistic in the goals it guides the reader toward, and easy to follow. If any author of books on health and fitness is qualified, she certainly is. Few can say "I rebuilt myself from the bottom up. I'm proof of what can be done. Let me share with you how to benefit from my experience!"

Deb Hirschhorn

This is an excerpt from an article I wrote on May 11, 2015 for a local newspaper in which I have a column. The article was about not making excuses in life:

My friend, Sharon Rawitz, was struck with several medical problems including a stroke. She went from being active in the community, a school counselor, and a ballet dancer and teacher to being unable to talk, walk, read, or write. But she had a will, a desire to live a complete and full life. I learned today that the Hebrew word, "will," *(ratzon)*, has the word "*rutz*" run, in it. Will is to want something so badly you run for it. Sharon ran toward health. Against all predictions that she would remain a vegetable, she willed herself to walk, talk, read, and write again. She even is teaching herself violin these days. And yes, she is back to teaching dancing lessons in her studio.

We need to desire Truth. Sharon could have adopted the rationalization that it is hard to fight a complete physical breakdown. Well, it certainly is. But the truth is that it is possible nevertheless. Falsehood would have been to say that it is impossible.

--Dr. Deb Hirschhorn, Ph.D.
Author of The Healing Is Mutual:
Marriage Empowerment Tools to Rebuild Trust and Respect -- Together

Nina Fleischman

Thinking about Sharon Rawitz and this worthwhile endeavor...a book about her journey to health after a life-changing physical challenge.

It was nothing short of a shock to hear when Sharon was stricken...a stroke, of all things!

Sharon was fit, healthy and active. She was involved in many activities: her work as a counselor in a New York City public school, as a mother, grandmother, world traveler, a dancer....and the list goes on.

Sharon always exuded joy and enthusiasm in anything she was doing, be it a walk, a swim on the beach, tending her garden, or talking about creative ways to engage her students in a new project.

Sharon Joy; a middle name befitting her demeanor.

Throughout her ordeal and recovery, even when I first visited her at a New York hospital, she was always upbeat and positive. It seemed that the worst was over, with diagnosis and treatment, and she was working and ready to take each new step, one step at a time, to recover her speech and movement. She demonstrated the same joy and determination to succeed as she always did. I remember when we sat in a garden at the hospital during that same visit, and she walked me through her experience to that point. With halting speech, she taught me to be patient while listening, and giving her time to express her words. A smile...a giggle...she made me more comfortable being with her.

It was being with the same joyful Sharon, with her easy, beautiful smile. She never expressed fear or frustration. She never bemoaned her fate. She only eagerly moved forward, to rehabilitate herself. She was motivated by therapists working with her, and she shared some of the speech and movement exercises that helped her.

Well, she has always been an inspiration to me...before...during...and now after her ongoing recovery. She lives on, with the utmost grace.

Interview:

Naomi Herzberg interviews Sharon Rawitz, January 22, 2014

An assignment towards Master's Degree in Adult Learning

"The Creative Mind and Wisdom During the Aging Process"

I conducted an interview of a highly creative (retired dance teacher) senior citizen, stroke victim, presently in the recuperation stage. I found that she was able to start the process of reaffirmation and discovering modalities from experiential learning, processed with intelligence, and applied in new ways, with God's help, which would allow her to continue her road to complete recovery. The aspects that she related to me had to do with: (1) Absolute need for a positive outlook and attitude -- she explained to me her deep understanding of what happened to her and the way she overcame these difficulties one step at a time. She literally had to take baby steps. This required her to continuously be positive and focus on the good. Her attitude was upbeat, which was quite difficult, as she was unable to use one side of her body. The mere fact that she was in her old life a dance teacher with a professional studio of her own, and now needed to teach herself how to walk, was traumatic. She was only able to accomplish this by continually associating with positive people. She tried to focus on her intelligence, which she still knew that she had. Her determination was amazing and a lesson for all. She also listened to dance music and tried to sing as well as speak. This was extremely difficult for her. She was very hopeful and prayed that one day she would get back to her old self. (2) Finding humor in difficult situations– It is not an easy thing to do. The way that she was able to handle this had to do with her previous experiential, hands-on learning situations. She had to deal with other sick people in her family and friendship circles. She also developed a sense of humor earlier on in life from various stages of her life that were not always so pleasant. She had learned early on in life that you need to laugh. Laughter had become a remedy for her when she was raising her children. This ability to find humor in difficult situations was an important factor that she felt had to be shared with me. She explained to me how pathetic it really was when she could not tie her shoes, lift a fork or spoon to feed herself, or close a zipper. The feeling was so devastating that she had no choice; either she would have to laugh or have to cry. I was extremely impressed with her honesty. Laughing at yourself and finding humor in each scenario that turned out strange, became funny in her eyes. This kept her going until improvement set in. What a relief! (3) Relearn fine motor and gross motor coordination--The situation was so bad that she needed to go for physical therapy on a regular basis, a few times a week. There were numerous problems involved in orchestrating this. First of all, she could not drive, so how was she getting there? Since her divorce she lived alone and did not have a person to go with her. She was not able to speak clearly, so giving instructions to a driver was difficult to do. Life certainly was not a bed of roses. What was a person in such a situation supposed to do for herself? I was fascinated by her story and spent an enormous amount of time with her, trying to guess what she would reveal to me, about each baby step that she took, before she actually did. I was expecting deep and mysterious answers to the many questions that I presented her with. Instead, I received straight and practical advice on how one should always reaffirm their position by discovering modalities from experiential learning. She explained how using your intelligence and tapping into one's ability for creativity she was able to plunge forward. She thanked G-d a million times for saving her life and made promises to herself that she would overcome this. Her creative juices in her head were working overtime. I learned a very important lesson from this part of the interview. Never give up has become a motto, which I have shared many times with those who would listen! (4) Re-learn visual, auditory and speech control - Was another area that needed to be dealt with. She had so many issues that needed to be addressed, that one wonders how it was possible! This was quite a battle for her. She was unable to see out of her eyes at all times. She had a very difficult time focusing on any object for too long a period. The strain on her body in itself was tiring. The possibility of correcting all these deficits played on her psyche immensely. Would she ever regain all of her capacities? The many questions that she asked the doctors and physical therapists that worked with her were unanswerable at times. Did the doctors really expect her to recuperate and get back to normal completely? She was determined to succeed, and succeed she did. While explaining the many steps that she took in order to correct all these crucial problems, I watched the happy look on her face. With each accomplishment she smiled in a way that I have never witnessed before. There was a feeling of contentment that radiated from her. How was it possible for her to get to the point that she was at today? She is a wonderful human being with a tremendous will to live normally. I am proud to be her friend and confidant. She somehow figured it all out. She went for all kinds of therapy with the help of an organization that aids people living with her set of circumstances.

The emotional affect on the stroke victim was very difficult to observe. She did an enormous amount of covering up. She so badly wanted to be looked at as 100% normal. I could feel the pain that she was suffering from. She was so busy trying to be upbeat that she forgot that she was a stroke victim. Her discussions with me turned out to be about the medical terms and treatments involved for stroke victims. It was as if she had nothing to do with it. I soon realized that this was her defense mechanism that worked for her. She was so eager to share with me her eagerness to survive normally: (1) To fight for good health - And fight it was. It was more than a fight, it was a revolutionary battle. There were no boundaries that she did not cross. With every ounce of strength she fought for all the help that she could receive. Determination and persistence were the names of the games. The only way that she could possibly win this war was to win it in its entirety. She was not taking any chances. Her will to be complete once again was her saving grace. The adrenaline that kept her going is what saved her in the end. When I asked her how this was possible, when all odds were against her, she answered me in a stern and strict voice - "there is no other way and she would not take no for an answer"! I could not believe how determined she was. I knew that my friend was tough but did not realize to what extent. She said that her mind was working over-time. It was then, that I realized, whatever she would have to do, would get done. She was going to overcome it all. I asked her what she meant by the statement, her mind was working overtime. She told me that she felt a rush in her head; brain cells being nourished constantly; and knew that with a healthy brain she would make it out of the forest, during her inner battle. It was this answer that made me realize it all; I too believed that she would. What a lesson on how emotions work in our behalf. (2) A desire to be an active member of society - Is a very important part of this equation. It was not enough for her to just recuperate. She did not want to have any residual affect left. She also wanted to be able to return to her position in the community, where she lived, as an active member. She was once a beloved dance teacher that taught many children in the neighborhood how to do ballet dancing. She had put on dance recitals with these children, that she sorely missed doing. Her intent was to be able to return to her old spaces and once again be an active member. She attended lectures and classes, once she was able to get around more. She made sure that her wardrobe was up to par. Her meticulous old grooming methods were once again put back in place. She insisted on returning to her old passions, such as gardening. Her garden was replanted by her, with beautiful flowers that sprouted in the spring, fall and summer. She painted her porch by herself and attended to repairs that needed to be done around her home. She started practicing once again in her ballet studio, located in the basement of her home. Slowly she began to regain her abilities, as she promised herself she would. She was reaffirming her abilities through actual doing. Her life experiences had certainly served her well. The creative juices were obviously still active, providing her with new wisdom. (3) A desire to share wisdom- Was a very definite part of her recuperation plan. There was not a subject that we spoke about which she did not relate to. Her knowledge was very thorough on almost every topic that I brought up. I was wondering if there were any losses of memory that she might have had due to the stroke. I did not notice any shortcomings. I found this to be an amazing situation. How was it possible to have a stroke and to recuperate so wonderfully? She maintained an enormous desire to share stories, narrations and her wisdom with me. My friend was working hard in all areas that required brain power to work. I realized in the process of speaking with her, that she wanted so badly to be validated as a contributing member of society, in action and in words. I started asking her advice, which she offered extensively. I realized that she was testing her own abilities to process information, as she thought carefully before answering any of my questions. Her answers were highly intelligent ones. I could tell that her mind was working, as she was exact in her answers. Her knowledge base was on an extremely sophisticated level. In no way could she have made up any of the answers to the particular medical and creative questions that she was asked. Her creative juices that nourish the brain were definitely still supplying the brain with nourishment. What a positive ending to a serious and unfortunate situation! (4) A discussion with the stroke victim on Alzheimer's disease, the MRI test, Neuroscience, brain aging and attitude--We thoroughly discussed her experiences from a medical perspective. She was able to share with me a blow by blow report of each and every aspect of her experiences and treatments. She spoke about how these tests were administered and by whom. She was cognizant of each and every fact. I was surprised at the level of understanding that she had. She explained to me what each test was about and administrated. She also was able to share an enormous amount of facts with me. She spoke about the MRI test in particular and the imaging. She talked about the battery of tests that she underwent that observed her verbal and nonverbal skills. She spoke about evaluations in a deep and knowledgeable manner. I received a very strong message from her, which is that she understood everything that was accomplished for her betterment, from a medical standpoint. After she received all the results of her tests, she first needed to develop a deep trust in G-d so that she could deal realistically with all her issues. She did accomplish this. It was only because of her deep belief and positive attitude that she was able to deal with all of it. There is not a chance that her brain is not working the same as it was beforehand. I, therefore conclude, the creative juices are still present and working.

Proven observational documentation accomplished through the interview process that creative juices do not deteriorate during the aging process in a senior citizen, despite being a stroke victim can be ascertained because: (1) Higher Awareness and great wisdom was present - Each time that I thought a negative response would turn up, it was just the opposite. The stroke victim interviewed was able to answer every question with specific details and explanations. She had an intense desire to be considered intelligent and knowledgeable. This was an easy message for me to have received, as that is exactly what she was. There is no doubt in my mind, that all of her past experiences and accomplishments worked in her favor.

She consistently drew strength from the reservoirs of information, which were stored away deep inside her brain. She was an inspiration for me as well as for my entire family, which have been getting to know her in a unique way. What a breath of fresh air. I am in complete awe of this wonderful lady that really knows what is important in life. Her appreciation for adult learning shows no bounds. Her appreciation for the beauty of life and the world at large is an important message to share with all. There is never room for negativity and therefore, we must always look at things in a positive light. I am convinced that in so doing, we have some input into shaping our destiny. She has displayed this in all the higher awareness and wisdom that was present. (2) Imagination and mind development was still functioning. At all times during the interview there was never a beat that she missed. I was certain that it would not be so. How is it possible to have gone through so much and not have a moment of silence? She was eager to share with me many creative thoughts on art, music, dance, social work, literature, flower arranging, raising children, organizational skills, learning styles, cognitive development, flexibility, imagination and so on. It became even clearer to me that this stroke victim was a superstar. Her imaginative thinking process was extremely interested in this interview, necessary for this project and paper. She has served as a tremendous asset to me. She has become a living example to me, in my preparation and research, needed for this literature review. What I also found fascinating was her ability to experiment with mind development skills, as we spoke about new topics along the way. She was able to speak about theories of development in both children and adults of all ages. It was at that time that she reminded me that she also held a master's degree in Counseling Psychology/Education. She had once worked as a guidance counselor and was very well versed in this area. Her memory was completely attuned to what we were talking about. What a wonderful opportunity it granted me towards the understanding of human relations. I consider myself to be fortunate. (3) Problem solving ability was present--Once I realized that there was no way that she could be trapped in any shape or form, I decided to take full advantage of her wisdom. I asked numerous questions that I needed help with in the form of problem solving. It was easy for her to come up with solutions and resolutions for any problem. I could not believe how feisty and anxious she was to contribute anything that she could to the success of my literature review. She was completely steeped with depth in the studies that I was sharing with her. She possessed an enormous thirst for more new knowledge. We sat and talked for hours and hours. She admitted to me that this type of conversation was one which she had not had in a long time; she was extremely grateful that I was including her in my literature review. She stated that as important as it is for me, it is even more important for her. That comment granted me tremendous satisfaction; it felt good to hear it from her. We have bonded and become much closer because of this, which is an added bonus. I have since been calling her and asking her many more problem solving ideas. She never seems to fail in the imagination department. Her creative thinking skills are totally up to par and maybe even better than the average person. The lessons that I have learned from her problem solving abilities have no measure. It's great! (4) Thesis statement reaffirmed--The creative mind sharpened with experience, knowledge and its innate flexibility to achieve higher awareness, may/ may not lose some of its creative juices and ability during the aging process; this will/ will not enhance our ability to gain more wisdom as we age.

"As long as the creative brain is not debilitated by illness and as long as society recognizes the value in contributions made by the elderly artist, there is no reason why a life cannot be filled to the brim with creative expression. As George Herbert once proclaimed,"

And now in age I bud again". Creativity can be regenerative. It is only our crystallized attitudes and our huge misconceptions about aging that cause us to think in terms of prime and decline. Society's low expectations for the "past the prime" years may have a negative effect by restricting or even stifling creativity more then we realize. If the human mind is its own fountain of youth, there is no limit on the beauty that can spring from it any age" (Bickhardt, 2003, p. 1).

Medical Records

Sharon Spring 2005 Peninsula Hospital Scans

April 15—negative CAT scan: no stroke, bleeding, tumor.

April 23—negative CAT scan—same as above.

April 24—MRI brain: enhancing lesion in the pons (Middle of the brain)—this is either inflammation or a small infarct (stroke). There could be underlying vasculitis although this is rare. There is also sinusitis of the right maxillary sinus (right side of face under your eye), and ethmoid sinusitis on both sides (just above your eyes).

April 24—MRA (magnetic resolution angiogram of the brain) -questionable narrowing (within the resolution limits of the machine which is the best MR machine available) of the two arteries feeding the middle of the brain. The arteries supplying the brain and those that feed that front and back of the brain are normal.

April 27—MRI cervical spine (neck)—No lesions in the spinal cord or the bones.

April 28—Carotid Doppler (the four vessels in the neck that feed the brain)—Negative

May 2--- MRI Brain Two completely new acute lesions in the left-brain. They could be infection, inflammatory, or blood vessel blockage.

Glossary

Part 1

Aphasia - Partial or total loss of the ability to articulate ideas or comprehend spoken or written language, resulting from damage to the brain caused by injury or disease. --from dictionary.com

Apraxia of speech, also known as verbal apraxia or dyspraxia, is a speech disorder in which a person has trouble saying what he or she wants to say correctly or consistently or correctly. It is not due to weakness or paralysis of the speech muscles [the muscles of the face, tongue, and lips]. The severity of speech can range from mild to severe. – From National Institutes of Health

Bikur Cholim Organization - a Jewish community supported charitable organization helping the sick and needy in the community

Chocolate egg cream soda – chocolate et crème soda (from the French) consists of chocolate syrup, cream or milk, and seltzer (no egg)

Hatzala - the volunteer communal ambulance

Kugel – pudding

Mensch - a decent human being, (soulful and kind)

MRA - magnetic resonance of arteries

MRI - magnetic resonance imaging used in detecting structural abnormalities of the body

Neshumah – soul

Rabbi – Jewish clergyman

RUSK – the rehabilitation center of New York University Medical Hospital

Siddur - a prayer book

Part 2

Bocce – Italian style bowling game

Bonnie Prudden – author of *Pain Erasure the Bonnie Prudden Way: erase pain in minutes without drugs with trigger point therapy*

Chavrusa - teacher and learning partner

Doctor of Osteopathy - a D.O. doctor is a medical doctor who specializes in correcting alignment with a combination of physical therapy and chiropractic

MRI –magnetic resonance imaging used in detecting structural abnormalities of the body

OBM – of blessed memory

Ohashiatsu Method – shiatsu method described in *The Ohashi Bodywork Book*

Oral Torah - is the *how*-to book that God taught Moses

Parsha - portion of the Torah that was read during the religious service

Shabbos – Jewish Sabbath, a day of spiritual energizing and physical day of rest

Shiur - a lecture, on a topic generally relating to the parsha or portion of the Torah that was read during the religious service

Shul – Jewish house of worship and learning; synagogue

Torah – a guide given by God and written down by the prophet Moses for people to grow and become mature human beings capable of partnering with God

Yeshiva - Orthodox Jewish school

www.ingramcontent.com/pod-product-compliance
Lightning Source LLC
Chambersburg PA
CBHW051409070526
44584CB00023B/3349